W9-AIS-247

It's All about God's Love

*A Retired Pastor Reflects on the
Sacrament of Reconciliation*

WILLIAM T. KREMMELL

WESTBOW
PRESS®
A DIVISION OF THOMAS NELSON
& ZONDERVAN

Copyright © 2019 William T. Kremmell.

All rights reserved. No part of this book may be used or reproduced by
any means, graphic, electronic, or mechanical, including photocopying,
recording, taping or by any information storage retrieval system
without the written permission of the author except in the case of
brief quotations embodied in critical articles and reviews.

Scripture texts in this work are taken from the New American Bible, revised
edition © 2010, 1991, 1986, 1970 Confraternity of Christian Doctrine,
Washington, D.C. and are used by permission of the copyright owner. All
Rights Reserved. No part of the New American Bible may be reproduced
in any form without permission in writing from the copyright owner.

WestBow Press books may be ordered through booksellers or by contacting:

WestBow Press
A Division of Thomas Nelson & Zondervan
1663 Liberty Drive
Bloomington, IN 47403
www.westbowpress.com
1 (866) 928-1240

Because of the dynamic nature of the Internet, any web addresses or
links contained in this book may have changed since publication and
may no longer be valid. The views expressed in this work are solely those
of the author and do not necessarily reflect the views of the publisher,
and the publisher hereby disclaims any responsibility for them.

Any people depicted in stock imagery provided by Getty Images are
models, and such images are being used for illustrative purposes only.
Certain stock imagery © Getty Images.

Cover art: The Prodigal's Return by John Byam Liston Shaw

ISBN: 978-1-9736-5525-1 (sc)
ISBN: 978-1-9736-5526-8 (e)

Library of Congress Control Number: 2019902740

Print information available on the last page.

WestBow Press rev. date: 03/19/2019

Dedicated to the women in my life
who have loved me, taught me, challenged me,
encouraged me, and supported me
throughout my life, as I have struggled to be
a faithful Christian and a genuine human being.

A special dedication to my sister, Ann Fowler,
who is one of the best priestly people I know.

Dedicated to the women in my life
who have loved me, taught me, challenged me,
encouraged me, and supported me
throughout my life, as I have struggled to be
a faithful Christian and a genuine human being.

A special dedication to my sister, Ann Fowler,
who is one of the best priestly people I know.

Contents

Introduction

I was ordained a Roman Catholic priest for the Archdiocese of Boston in 1966. I had grown up in a very Catholic environment in the 1940s and 50s, participating in all things Catholic, including regular Mass and Confession. I enjoyed strong Catholic influences, including my loving Catholic parents, my devoted parish priests, and the dedicated sisters in our local parochial school. I was an altar server from a young age, enthralled by the liturgical rituals and symbols (the smells and bells), the otherworldly Gregorian chant, and especially the solemnity of Christmas, Holy Week, and Easter. These influences were seeds of my vocation to the priesthood.

Going back to those "good old days," I have vivid memories of Saturday Confession at a time when large numbers of people came to the Sacrament every week. I remember waiting in line in the lower church, rehearsing over and over what I would say to the priest, worrying that I would forget something that would invalidate my confession, and fearing that the priest would recognize my voice and call me by name. It was a somewhat intimidating experience, hardly an encounter with a loving God.

I prepared for the priesthood at St. John's Seminary in Brighton, Massachusetts, during the days before, during, and after the Second Vatican Council. Part of my seminary routine was to meet regularly with a confessor, one of the seminary faculty members. It was a rather routine affair; I don't remember it being a particularly uplifting spiritual experience. After ordination, I continued to approach the

Sacrament of Penance (as it was called in those days) without much enthusiasm. I did it because I was a priest who taught the importance of the Sacrament, and I wanted to lead by example.

As the years went on, I approached the Sacrament less and less frequently. It just didn't make sense for me to confess basically the same litany of sins again and again, without feeling that I was growing any closer to the Lord. My confessor offered sincere but generic spiritual pep talks, but he didn't motivate me to want to overcome my selfish tendencies. For a period of time, I stopped going to Confession altogether. But happily, I never stopped thinking about the Sacrament: what it was supposed to be as a sign of God's merciful and healing love, how much I needed to experience that love in a concrete way, and what needed to change in me to make it happen. Finally, after much prayer and reflection, I came back to the Sacrament, not as a weekly or monthly routine, but as a grace-filled encounter with my loving God in preparation for Christmas and Easter, during my annual retreat, and on other special occasions.

As I returned to Reconciliation and began to experience it as a positive spiritual experience, I started giving talks to parents, as they prepared their young children to receive the Sacrament of Reconciliation for the first time. I talked about the reality of sin in our lives, how we must not ignore it, and how I personally came to the realization that I absolutely need the healing power of God to enable me to overcome the stronghold that temptation and sin can exert over me. I acknowledged that many people had bad experiences in the past, as we focused too much on how bad we were as sinners and not enough on how good God is, the God who loves us as we are and wants to help us to achieve our full spiritual potential. I underscored the fact that the Sacrament is meant to be *all about God's love for us*!

In more recent years, I have given talks about the Sacrament of Reconciliation at retreats, parish missions, evenings of prayer, and other programs of adult spirituality. And guess what! People not only told me that my talks helped them (One retreatant said, "I wish I had known you thirty years ago"), but they also encouraged me to put my reflections down in printed form. Hence, I was inspired to write the book you have before you.

I have written this book because I am concerned about the moral climate in our society today. We've lost a healthy sense of sin, a sense of right and wrong, a sense of objective morality. Many of our young people are floundering, adrift without a moral anchor. And many adults, especially elders, have rejected the guilt-ridden experiences of the past, without replacing them with some new, positive, spiritually uplifting experience of God's forgiving love here and now.

I have written this book to help my fellow Catholics (clergy and laity) appreciate that we are all sinners; that, at times, we can be self-righteous, self-centered, and self-serving; and that we need to acknowledge this in a healthy, not a morbid, way. I also want to underscore the truth that God loves us in our sinfulness and is with us, not to condemn us, but to help us overcome our selfish tendencies and to draw closer to his love. I believe that God greatly desires that we experience him in the Sacrament of Reconciliation.

I have written this book because so few Catholics approach the Sacrament of Reconciliation these days. They are turned off by the way the Sacrament has been offered in the past and have not found any new motivation to approach the Sacrament today. They haven't got the message that it's all about God's love. Unfortunately, many Church leaders have not gotten the message either. I have written this book to help them reimagine the Sacrament.

This book is my personal reflection on what I believe has and has not been helpful with the way we have celebrated the Sacrament (even with the revised ritual) and what might be helpful to further renew the Sacrament, so that it will have a more positive focus as a sign of God's unconditional and boundless love. I would like to think that I am a loyal son of the Church and that any criticisms or suggestions for renewal that I make in this book come out of my love for the Church and my hope that the powerful Sacrament of

Reconciliation will be renewed and restored to its important place in our spiritual life.

I offer thanks to the many people who have encouraged me to write this book, especially pastoral ministers with whom I have worked. Special thanks to the people I have run into during the past couple of years, especially former parishioners, who have asked me, "How is the book coming? People are waiting to read it." I sense that they have been instruments of the Holy Spirit, moving me to complete the task. I also want to thank the people who have read all or sections of the book, offering affirmation and helpful suggestions.

One of the things I have learned from the experience of putting my thoughts down on paper is that I am not a natural writer. Writing this book has been a long, slow slog for me. I often asked myself, "Why are you torturing yourself with this project?" Now that the book is done, I hope that at least some people will find it to be a helpful tool in deepening their relationship with our loving and merciful God.

> **Note:** In writing this book, I have tried to be inclusive in my language about God, but I have not always been successful. I have struggled to use words to describe God that speak to the fullness of who God is, but sometimes I have found it to be awkward in writing about a personal God without using personal terms. I ask forgiveness for where I have failed.

CHAPTER 1
God's Love Is Everlasting ... Really!

God loves us totally, unconditionally, always,
and in all ways—with no exceptions.

A popular comedian who often criticized organized religion once had this to say:

> Religion has actually convinced people that there is an invisible man living in the sky, who sees everything you do, and commands you to follow a special list of ten things, or he'll send you to a place of fire, smoke, death, and crying forever and ever—but he loves you.

This is a sad description of God that has, in many ways, been handed down by many sincere religious leaders to many sincere people of faith. Happily, as one prominent religious leader has assured us, "God is bigger than religion."

"God is love." That is what St. John tells us in his first letter (John 4:8). God *is* love, which is different from saying that God loves. God's very nature is love. God is the embodiment of love, the fullness of love, and total self-giving. The God who is love reveals

1

God's love in the person of Jesus Christ. Jesus told us, "No one has greater love than this, to lay down one's life for one's friends" (John 15:13). And Jesus did it. In his years of ministry and in his passion and death, he laid down his life for all people, and that includes you and me. If you remember nothing else from this book, remember this: God loves you, and God loves everyone unconditionally, always, and in all ways—no exceptions.

The scriptures use many images to tell us about God's love. For example, in the Psalms, God is described as "a stronghold in time of trouble" (Ps. 9); "my strength, my rock, my fortress, my deliverer" (Ps. 18); "my shepherd" (Ps. 23); "my light and my salvation" (Ps. 27); "my strength and my shield" (Ps. 28); "my helper" (Ps. 30); and "my shelter from distress" (Ps. 32). Grounded in the love of God, we will not be shaken, no matter what comes; we will find strength and safety in all the circumstances of our lives.

In chapter 31 of the book of the prophet Jeremiah, God reassures us, "I have loved you with an everlasting love; therefore I have continued my faithfulness to you."

There is a popular refrain that is spoken or sung at Sunday mass between verses of a responsorial psalm: "God's love is everlasting." We pray it, but do we truly believe it? Do we believe what the letter to the Romans says to us regarding God's constant love?

> What will separate us from the love of Christ? Will anguish, or distress, or persecution, or famine, or nakedness, or peril, or sword? No, in all these things we conquer overwhelmingly through him who loved us. For I am convinced that neither death, nor life, nor angels, nor principalities, nor present things, nor future things, nor powers, nor height, nor depth, nor any other creature will be able to separate us from the love of God in Christ Jesus our Lord. (Rom. 8:35, 37–39)

God even loves us in our sinfulness. When we worship the false gods of money (the almighty dollar) and material things (our modern version of the golden calf) and make them our priority, *God still loves us.* When we reject the Sabbath as the Lord's day, which is a holy day and a day of rest every week, *God still loves us.* When we don't love our neighbors as we love ourselves; when we don't love as Jesus loves, which is selflessly and unconditionally; when we don't respect the sanctity of all human life; when we are indifferent to the genuine needs of those whose lives are jeopardized by lack of nutritious food, adequate housing, clean water, and medical care; and when we ignore our neighbor who is sick, suffering, lonely, depressed, and left out, *God still loves us.*

Yes, God's love is everlasting. Do you believe it?

A cartoon depicts a pastor in the pulpit saying, "Today I am going to speak about the Ten Commandments, or as they are now called, the ten loose guidelines." When we treat God's commandments or Jesus's beatitudes as loose guidelines, *God still loves us.*

Through the years, I have come across many quotes that speak to me of the reality of God's boundless love, including the following:

- I love you just the way you are. (Billy Joel) It sounds like God to me.
- God loves us as we are and not as we should be. (Brennan Manning)
- God loves us, not because we are good; God loves us because God is good. (Richard Rohr OFM)
- There is nothing we could do to make God love us any less. (Arise International Program video)

Echoing the words of the Roman Catholic marriage vows, God loves us in good times and in bad, in spiritual sickness or in health. God promises to love us and honor us all the days of our lives. Many people I talk to find God's unconditional love hard to understand or accept. "How can God love that so-and-so?" "How can God love me after what I've done?"

God wants to make sure we get his message of unconditional love, so he sent his only Son to reveal God's love in word and deed. The four gospels are filled with indications of how much God loves us. Early on in St. John's gospel (John 3:16–17), Jesus says,

> God so loved the world that he gave his only Son, so that everyone who believes in Him might not perish but might have eternal life. For God did not send his son into the world to condemn the world, but that the world might be saved through him.

That's a whole lot of loving (not condemning) going on through the person of Jesus. The gospels describe Jesus as the shepherd (leading us), as the light (enlightening us), as the bread of life (nourishing us), and as the vine (enlivening us). All of these are indications of his love for us. And the letter to the Romans (Rom. 5:8) reminds us that God's love comes with an unconditional guarantee. "God proves his love for us in that while we were still sinners, Christ died for us." Before we could 'fess up and shape up, Christ died for us as the ultimate act of love.

In my personal life, Jesus has often spoken to me of his love through the words of special people. I remember a woman in one of my earliest parishes who, as she greeted me after Mass, would always say, "You are so special." Initially, I felt uncomfortable at her affirmation. But gradually, as weeks and months went by, I began to appreciate her greeting as words of love—words that reflected God's own affirming love for me. I also remember a spiritual director who, when I shared my spiritual struggles with her, would respond, "Bill, God really delights in you." When she spoke so simply and so genuinely, I sensed God really delighting in me. On countless occasions during my fifty-plus years as a priest, Jesus has reassured me that he loves me, and he communicates that love through special people in special circumstances.

Yes, our God speaks words of love in many striking and sometimes surprising ways. God also reveals love in mighty deeds, such as healing, feeding, comforting, reassuring, and enlivening us through the acts of total sacrifice we see in his followers. I think of my married sister who, with the support of her husband, spent weeks with me, attending to my every need on two different occasions after major surgeries. Through people like my sister, God acts with love today as God acted with love in ages past. God is always hoping that we will get the message of love and that we will want to enter into a more intimate relationship with the God who is love.

We usually think of the season of Advent as a time of waiting for some new manifestation of God with us. We don't usually think of God as always in an Advent mode, always waiting for us to come and enter into a deep bond of love. Jesus invites us. "Come to me, all you who labor and are burdened, and I will give you rest" (Matt. 11:28). In the book of Revelation, God says, "Behold, I stand at the door and knock. If anyone hears my voice, and opens the door, then I will enter his house and dine with him and he with me" (Rev. 3:20). I am reminded of the first verse of the popular hymn "Table of Plenty," by Dan Schutte, where God says, "O come and sit at my table where saints and sinners are friends. I wait to welcome the lost and lonely, to share the cup of my love."

God's love is everlasting!

Since the earliest days of my ministry as a Roman Catholic priest, I have always felt confident that God has called me to the priesthood, but I have questioned whether I was called to be celibate. (I have felt a strong pull toward married life.) I have also questioned whether celibacy, a church discipline, needs to be a sine qua non for ordination to the priesthood. After all, Eastern rite Catholic priests can be married. Married Episcopal priests who become Roman Catholics can apply for the Catholic priesthood. And of course, we had married priests and bishops in the earliest centuries of our Western church.

In the mid-1980s, I developed a beautiful and appropriate friendship with a woman who lived in a parish where I was serving. She reflected God's love for me in her loving spirit. When it became clear to me that the relationship was growing deeper, I began thinking that I should take a leave of absence to explore the relationship apart from priestly ministry. I went on an eight-day directed retreat at a Jesuit retreat house on the coast of Gloucester, Massachusetts, to step aside and pray for God's guidance.

I entered into deep dialogue (prayer) with Jesus for eight days. I thought, *Should I stay as a celibate priest and end the relationship, or should I leave active ministry to explore the relationship more freely?* One thing was clear: I was not going to deepen the relationship while functioning as a priest. So, I prayed, *"Loving God, what do you want me to do?"*

Now I was beginning to feel guilty. If I took the leave, would I be turning away from my commitment to Jesus and his ministry? Would I be disappointing and even hurting Jesus from a human perspective? Would I be committing sin?

As the retreat was drawing to an end, I intensified my prayer: "Jesus, what should I do? I want to explore the relationship, but I don't want to abandon you. I don't want to jeopardize my relationship with you. I don't want to lose your love." Then and there I sensed Jesus speaking to me: "Yes, I need you as a priest. You are a loving and compassionate minister of my good news. You bring special gifts to my people. But I created you fully human, fully alive. I know your needs. I want you to feel free to explore whatever will be fulfilling, whatever will make you truly happy. No matter what you decide, *I will still love you with the fullness of my love.*" So I took a leave. Yes, God's love is everlasting.

I think of the wonderful reflection on love in the first letter to the Corinthians. Since God is love, we can rightly substitute the name *God* for the word *love* in the reading, and it will read like this: "God is patient; God is kind; God is not envious or boastful or arrogant or rude. God does not insist on God's own way; God is not irritable or resentful; God does not rejoice in wrongdoing, but rejoices in the truth. God bears all things, believes all things, hopes all things, endures all things. God's love never ends."

God has certainly been patient with me in my struggles. God has not insisted on God's own way (God gave me the freedom to take my leave). God has put up with a lot of my selfishness, foolishness, and sin. As I continue to struggle to be a faithful disciple, I believe that God will love me no matter where I am or what I do. Do you believe that our God loves you and will always love you in just that same way?

CHAPTER 2
And Then There's Sin!

We are all sinners, capable of
weakening or rupturing
our relationship with God and with others

In a wide-ranging interview six month after his election, Pope Francis was asked: "Who is Jorge Mario Bergoglio?" (This was his birth name.) And he answered: "I do not know what might be the most fitting description. I am a sinner. This is the most accurate definition. It is not a figure of speech, a literary genre. I am a sinner." His answer reminds me of something the nuns used to tell us in Catholic grammar school: "Even the pope goes to confession." They were telling us that we are all sinners, and we all need God's loving forgiveness! Sadly, many people in our secular society have lost a sense of sin.

So what is sin? The Catechism of the Catholic Church defines sin in this way: "Sin is an offense against reason, truth, and right conscience; it is failure in genuine love for God and neighbor caused by a perverse attachment to certain goods. It wounds the nature of man and injures human solidarity. It has been defined as 'an utterance, a deed, or a desire contrary to the eternal law'" (Liguori Publications, 1994, #1849). This definition is couched in "Church-speak"—that is, theological language—but at its heart, it seems to suggest that sin is a failure to love in our relationship with God and with our fellow human beings.

Pope Francis has pointed out that "we all have darkness in our lives … Walking in darkness means being overly pleased with ourselves, believing that we do not need salvation. That is darkness!" That is our sin. I think of the old TV commercial, where someone exclaims, "I'd rather do it myself." Once we conclude that we don't *need* God (or anyone else), that we don't need to be saved from our selfish tendencies, that we don't need real relationship, we can find ourselves walking in deeper darkness, and we deceive ourselves into thinking that the darkness is light. For example, I can purchase more and more of the latest technological wonders and convince myself that those instruments of communication will bring me ultimate happiness (light). But I will inevitably be disappointed, because only God is the source of true light and life.

Personally, I like to define sin in the context of the parable of the lost sheep (Luke 15:4–7). The shepherd and his flock of sheep have a real relationship. The shepherd knows each of his sheep in a personal way, and the sheep know their shepherd as a loving leader and provider. One of the sheep wanders off from the flock to do its own thing, to explore greener pastures, to experience a kind of "freedom." This lost sheep, through a selfish desire, weakens its relationship with the shepherd and distances itself from the flock. *This is sin—* weakening, wounding, and/or rupturing our relationship with the God who is our loving shepherd and with our brothers and sisters in the human family.

A healthy relationship is based on selfless love. "I want to be with you. I want to please you. I want to make sacrifices for you. I want to make a commitment to you. I want to be faithful to you." During my years of parish ministry, I found that many Catholics do not have a real relationship with God (Jesus). They know facts about Jesus. They know the doctrines and moral codes and rituals of his Church. They do what has to be done (often the minimal) to get to heaven. They fulfill their obligations (often out of fear), but they don't really know Jesus in a personal, relational way.

Sin presumes that we have a real relationship with God to begin with. Selfishly we can wander away from that relationship, as the lost sheep wandered away from the shepherd and the flock. In our humanness, we can easily wander and become distracted from our relationship with a loving God. We can be seduced and waylaid by the false gods of this world: money, material things, power, and prestige. We can gravitate toward the promise of instant gratification and satisfaction. We can be tempted to embrace a way of life that says: "It's all about me," a life in which we become self-absorbed, self-serving, and self-centered. We don't need God. As one of my classmates in the seminary put it, we take God for extra credit—that is, only when all else fails.

The story is told of a little girl, who was helping her father decorate the Christmas tree. As they were placing ornaments and tinsel on the tree, she suddenly asked her dad: "Why don't people pay attention to Jesus at Christmastime?" The father was understandably taken aback, and he asked her: "What makes you say a thing like that?" And the girl, without hesitation, answered: "Well, at Christmastime, everyone sings, 'O come let us ignore him!'" During the Christmas season, we Christians proclaim in song and story that Jesus is our Savior, that we have a real relationship with him. But to a great extent, we ignore him; we don't need him. We find our salvation in all the material trappings that have become the heart of Christmas and the heart of our lives. This can also be true in our daily living beyond Christmas.

Sadly, in our secular society today, sin often masquerades as good. For example, sometimes when I meet someone whom I haven't seen for a while, I'll ask, "How are you?" And frequently the reply will be, "I'm busy, thank God." Busyness and racing about have become virtues. We're exhausted with our schedule and our commitments, but "thank God." We're frazzled, bordering on being burnt out, but "thank God." In our busyness, we are affirmed as tireless workers or as committed activists in the community. We have no time for a day of rest every week (Sabbath), no time for prayer and reflection, no time to just *be*. That is our sin!

I am reminded of "The Howling Man," an episode on the classic TV series *The Twilight Zone*. In this powerful drama, a man named David Ellington finds himself caught in a terrible storm and seeks shelter at a local monastery. Once inside, he hears a wolf-like sound coming from somewhere in the building and is warned by the head of the religious community to stay away from the howling man who is locked in a cell. David is told that the prisoner is actually the devil.

David cannot resist the temptation to talk to the prisoner, who seems cultured and articulate and claims that he is a good person who is being held against his will. When David visits the man a second time, the prisoner convinces David that he is good, and it is the monks who are evil. Reluctantly, David lets the howling man out of his cell, and as the man walks down a long corridor, he is transformed into a satanic being, horns and all. He is indeed the devil.

David rushes to the head monk, explains what he did, and confesses, "I didn't recognize him." The monk, horrified at what David has said, responds, "That is the devil's strength and man's weakness." Yes, evil (sin) often masquerades as good. Embracing that deception is our weakness and our sin.

Every day we Christians face a war, a war between two different worlds we live in. There is a war going on between God's kingdom and the kingdom of this world in which we live, a war between the world of the Spirit and the world of the flesh (selfishness), a war between good and evil. In his letter to the Romans, St. Paul says,

> I do not do the good I want, but I do the evil I do
> not want. Now if I do what I do not want, it is no
> longer I who do it, but sin that dwells in me. So,
> then, I discover the principle that when I want to do
> right, evil is at hand. For I take delight in the law

11

of God, in my inner self, but I see in my members another principle at war with the law of my mind, taking me captive to the law of sin that dwells in my members. Miserable one that I am! (Romans 7:19–24)

Hopefully we want to live in God's kingdom. We want to live life in the Spirit. We want to follow the way of Jesus, *but* we also want to follow the way of this world. We like our creature comforts. We like our stuff, and we can easily be seduced into spending more time and focus on our stuff (like iPads, computers, etc.) than on the one true God. We pray the Lord's Prayer, unconsciously saying, as Father Richard Rohr suggests: "Thy kingdom come, but my kingdom stay." That is the war of the worlds. That selfish inclination is our sin.

Many people have lost a sense of sin altogether. They believe in their basic goodness, so they believe that whatever they do that is not good, God will understand it. Their theme song is the old romantic ballad, "You Light Up My Life," in which we sing, "It can't be wrong if it feels so right." Or they, in effect, proclaim lyrics from *West Side Story*, which suggest, "When love comes so strong, there is no right or wrong." Many senior citizens proudly tell me, "What do I do that's a sin at my age?" It's almost as if they've lost a sense of the basic selfishness that we all deal with in one way or another as human beings throughout our entire lives. For some people, their sin is their belief that there is no sin in them.

"I am a sinner," Pope Francis said. Hopefully we can say the same and turn to Jesus, our loving Savior, for healing and forgiveness.

CHAPTER 3
The God of Love in the World of Sinners

Jesus loves sinners
and wants to be close to us sinners

Jesus frequently speaks to me through the lyrics of popular songs. He has spoken clearly to me through this oldie but goodie by Irving Berlin, entitled "Always":

> I'll be loving you always. With a love that's true always. When the things you've planned need a helping hand, I will understand always.

In the first chapter of St. Matthew's Gospel, the angel of the Lord announces to Joseph that Mary, his fiancé, will give birth to a son, and according to the prophet, he shall be named Emmanuel, which means "God is with us." Our God loves us so much that God wanted to be with us in the flesh, wanted to assure us that he'll be with us always. As someone said, paraphrasing words from the prologue of St. John's Gospel: "The Word became flesh and moved into our neighborhood." Jesus wants to experience everything we experience, including temptation (think of his desert experience)— everything except sin.

During his earthly ministry, Jesus (Emmanuel) had a special relationship with sinners. He hung out with them. He ate with them. He wanted to be close to them. He wanted them to know: *God loves sinners! God forgives sinners!* In St. Mark's gospel (Mark 2:1–12), Jesus is accused of blasphemy for claiming that he could forgive the sins of a paralytic. He answered:

> "Why are you thinking such things in your hearts? Which is easier to say to the paralytic, 'Your sins are forgiven,' or to say, 'Rise, pick up your mat and walk?' But that you may know that the Son of Man has authority to forgive sins on earth"—he said to the paralytic, "I say to you, rise, pick up your mat, and go home."

Jesus is in effect telling us, "I am performing the exterior miracles of physical healing so that you may know that I have the power to perform the much deeper interior miracles, the healing of your broken, sinful spirit."

A little later in Mark 2:16–17, we read: "Some scribes who were Pharisees saw that he (Jesus) was eating with sinners and tax collector, and said to his disciples, 'Why does he eat with tax collectors and sinners?' Jesus heard this and said to them, 'Those who are well do not need a physician, but the sick do. I did not come to call the righteous but sinners.'" It is clear that sinners had a special place in Jesus's life. Jesus loves all sinners dearly and always.

Jesus came as the light of the world to banish the darkness of sin in the world. "The light shines in the darkness, and the darkness has not overcome it" (John 1:5). Jesus came as the good shepherd, to show us "the Way" to live a good life, not the empty life that masquerades as a good life. "The sheep follow him because they recognize his voice" (John 10:4). Jesus came as "the Truth" to rescue people from falsehood, when "they exchanged the truth of God for a lie" (Romans 1:25). Jesus came as "the Life" to save us from sin and eternal death. "I came so that they might have life and have it more abundantly" (John 10:10). Yes, Jesus loves us sinners and came to save us from darkness, from emptiness, from falsehood, from the death that is selfishness and sin.

The story of the Prodigal Son (Luke 15:11–32) is one of the most familiar of Jesus's parables and a powerful testament to God's love and mercy. A father had two sons. The younger son wanted to do his own thing, "to find himself," as young people today might say. He asked his father for his share of his inheritance, rather abruptly severed his relationship with his father, and off he went, to live what the gospel calls a life of dissipation, that is, a life of material excess and self-indulgence, what we might also call a life of selfishness and sin. He enjoyed his new life for some time until the money ran out. Unfortunately, he had no back-up resources. When a famine struck his country, he was hungry and was probably homeless. Now what was he to do?

Jesus continues the story: "Coming to his senses, he thought, 'How many of my father's hired workers have more than enough food to eat, but here I am, dying from hunger. I shall get up and go to my father and I shall say to him, 'Father, I have sinned against heaven and against you. I no longer deserve to be called you son; treat me as you would treat one of your hired workers.' So he got up and went back to his father" (Luke 15:17–20). It appears that the son was not truly sorry for hurting his father; his rehearsed speech seems to suggest that he was sorry for himself. At best, he made what the Church has called an imperfect act of contrition. At worst, there was no real sorrow at all.

During all the time the son was away, it seems clear that the father never stopped loving his son. He hoped and prayed that his son would return to him. Every day he looked out for any sign of his son coming home. The father's love for his son was unconditional. "I'll take him any way I can get him," he undoubtedly said to himself. "He is my son. I love him. I love him just the way he is, and I hope my love will make him better."

The story tells us: "While he was still a long way off, his father caught sight of him, and was filled with compassion." He probably saw how gaunt and bedraggled his son was, and was pained at the sight. The father "ran to his son, embraced him, and kissed him." Often, when I've given a teaching on this story, I'll ask my audience, "So what did the father say to his returning son?" After the people hem and haw for a minute or two, trying to come up with what the father said, I give them the answer: "The father said nothing. That's right. Nothing!" It would have been understandable, from a human perspective, if the father had expressed some anger or had questioned the son's intention for coming home. But instead the story reports that the father turned and spoke to his servants: "Quickly bring the finest robe and put it on him; put a ring on his finger and sandals on his feet. Take the fattened calf and slaughter it. Then let us celebrate with a feast, because this son of mine was dead and has come to life again; he was lost and has been found." The father's first impulse was: Let's celebrate! Later on he undoubtedly said to his son, "Let's talk and be reconciled."

I have been deeply moved by a painting entitled "The Prodigal's Return," by John Byam Liston Shaw (See the painting on the front cover). In it, the artist does not portray the reunion of father and son but rather focuses on the father, standing on the balcony of his home, looking out into the distance, searching for any sign of his wayward son. The father is faithful, hopeful, and full of love for his son. That is a powerful image of a loving God in the world of sinners. I don't know how this story came to be known as the parable of the prodigal son, when I believe Jesus is, first and foremost, trying to teach us about the loving father.

In *Webster's Collegiate Dictionary* (2004), the noun *prodigal* is first defined as "one who spends or gives lavishly and foolishly." In that sense, the father was a prodigal, since he gave his love to his son lavishly and some would say, foolishly. In the same way, our God is a prodigal God who loves us lavishly and foolishly in our good times and bad, in our goodness and our sin.

There are many contemporary images of the God who loves sinners. One of my favorites comes from *A Raisin in the Sun*, the 1959 play by Lorraine Hansberry. In this powerful drama, the husband and father of the Younger family has recently died, and Mama Lena receives a life insurance check for $10,000. Each member of the family has a dream as to what the money should be used for. Mama Lena puts a down payment on a new house. She entrusts the rest of the money to her son Walter, who makes a bad investment and loses it all, including the money that his sister Beneatha hoped she would have for her education.

Beneatha is angry and bitter, but Mama Lena, reflecting the unconditional love of God, initiates the following conversation with her daughter:

Mama, "I thought I taught you to love him."

Beneatha, "Love him? There is nothing left to love."

Mama, "There is always something left to love. And if you ain't learned that, you ain't learned nothing. Have you cried for that boy today? I don't mean for yourself and for the family 'cause we lost the money. I mean for him: what he been through and what it done to him. Child, when do you think is the time to love somebody the most? When they done good and made things easy for everybody? Well, then, you ain't through learning—because that ain't the time at all. It's when he's at his lowest and can't believe in hisself 'cause the world done whipped him so. When you starts measuring somebody, measure him right, child, measure him right. Make sure you done taken into account what hills and valleys he come through before he got to wherever he is." (A Signet Book, 1988)

The love of Lena for her son speaks to us of God's love for us, when we have weakened our relationship with God and with one another through our sin. God is there with us and for us at our lowest. God knows the hills and valleys we've been through and cries for us in our struggles. As someone once said, "We are all precious in the sight of God. He may shake his head a lot, but we're still precious." That is how I picture the God of love in the world of sinners

CHAPTER 4
Reconciliation: A Sure Sign of God's Love and Mercy

The focus of the *Sacrament* of *Reconciliation*
should be the healing, loving presence of Jesus.

Our loving and merciful God reveals God's love for us in many beautiful, wonderful, and often-surprising ways. We experience God in nature: in the warmth of the sun, in the power of the ocean, and in the bubbling of a woodland brook. We experience God touching us in a mighty wind and a gentle breeze. We experience God speaking to us in the chirping of birds at dawn and in the splash of colors on the horizon at dusk. We experience God in the grandeur of the mountains far off and in the intimate moments of awe at the sight of a playful critter in our own backyard.

We also experience God in the people who come into our lives, the people who affirm us, who challenge us, who encourage us to keep trying. We experience God in the child who gives us unconditional love, in the family member who points out our faults but loves us anyway, in the friend who is always there with a kind word or a reassuring gesture, in the neighbor or the parishioner who offers to help when we need it most. I think of the disabled man in the wheelchair at Mass, who gave me two thumbs up during my homily. I think of the children who have given me a hug or a

high-five or a homemade greeting card when I least expected it.
I think of the couple who traveled a thousand miles to be at my
installation as pastor in a new parish. I think of the woman who
spent the better part of a day helping me clean up my office and
challenging me to let go of lots of stuff I didn't need and probably
would never use again. I think of a priest who challenged me to leave
a parish ministry that was not a positive experience. I think of the
woman who greeted me after Mass, hugged me, and thanked me
for my joyful spirit, saying, "You are our parish joyologist." These
are just a few people, among countless people, who come to mind,
who have revealed to me the presence of a loving God as I journey
along the path of my life

One incident was particularly memorable. A dear friend Jodi
and I had a heated argument during Holy Week. I had said I would
lead an informal Easter sunrise service outside her home, if it didn't
rain. She insisted that we have the service no matter what the
weather turned out to be. We both got quite irritated, and we parted
company with some hard feelings in our hearts. The next morning,
the parish secretary informed me that a woman was waiting to see
me in my office. When I entered the office, there was my friend with
a bouquet of flowers, a big hug, and a word of apology. We enjoyed
a beautiful moment of healing and reconciliation, and when I think
back on the experience, I know that I also experienced the healing
love of Jesus in that encounter.

St. Ignatius, in his spiritual exercises, speaks about finding God
in all things. Yes, signs of God's love are everywhere, in everyone,
and in everything. Someone else expressed it this way: "The world
is pregnant with God." Through nature and people and a variety of
experiences, God's love is born anew into our lives.

And then there are the sacraments: seven sure signs of God's love
for us, with us, and in us. The old Baltimore Catechism defined a
sacrament as "an outward sign instituted by Christ to give grace." As
a child, I learned that definition and I memorized it, but I never really
understood what it meant. The definition in the new Catechism

of the Catholic Church is not much clearer: "The sacraments are perceptible signs (words and actions) accessible to our human nature. By the action of Christ and the power of the Holy Spirit they make present efficaciously the grace they signify" (#1084). I don't think that this language speaks clearly to the average Catholic Christian. So here is my personal definition of a sacrament, coming from fifty years of priestly ministry: "A sacrament is a visible sign, given to us by Jesus, to show us his abiding presence, his power, and his love." When we see the sign, whether it is water, oil, bread, or the laying of hands, we should be able to say, "Aha, Jesus is here with me. Jesus loves me!"

The sacraments coincide with significant moments or experiences in our lives, where Jesus wants to reveal his presence. Among those times are moments when we know that we have sinned and need spiritual healing and forgiveness. At those times, when we know we have hurt someone or have transgressed God's law of love, we may feel a deep sorrow, a sense of our human weakness, a guilt that weighs us down. In the Sacrament of Reconciliation (as we call it now), Jesus is welcoming us home. He is embracing us with the fullness of his love. He is offering us healing of our brokenness, unconditional forgiveness, and that peace the world cannot give.

Two Gospel incidents speak to me in a profound way about the Sacrament of Reconciliation. The first is the scene with Jesus and the woman taken in adultery (John 8:3–11). A woman is brought before Jesus and the crowd of people who were with him. She had committed the serious sin of adultery, a capital offense, deserving of death. The scribes and the Pharisees wanted to use her as an example to challenge Jesus's teaching on love and forgiveness. I can only imagine what she was feeling at that moment. She was undoubtedly ashamed of her sin. She was embarrassed, standing in the midst of all these people, her sinfulness exposed for all to see. And she was afraid that she was about to be executed. Jesus confronted the scribes and Pharisees in his own inimitable way. He exposed their own sinfulness, embarrassing them to the point that they all walked away.

Now the woman is left alone with Jesus. So how does he react to her? He doesn't question her about her sin. (Are you married? How many times did you commit adultery? With how many different men? And, while we're at it, what other sins have you committed? Be specific. Be complete.) He doesn't ask her if she is sorry. He doesn't make her feel guilty. He doesn't ask her what is her intention for the future. (Do you have a firm purpose of amendment?) He simply asks her, "Has no one condemned you?" She says, "No one, sir." And Jesus says, "Neither do I condemn you. Go, and from now on do not sin anymore." Jesus doesn't condemn her. Rather he forgives her and encourages her to avoid sin in the future. He gives her the gift of peace in her troubled heart. I can almost imagine Jesus giving her a great big, loving hug. For me, Jesus's response to the woman taken in adultery is how we as sinners are meant to experience Jesus in the Sacrament of Reconciliation.

The second incident that speaks to me of Jesus and his way of reconciliation happened on the night of the Resurrection, when Jesus met the apostles for the first time since his passion and death (John 20:19–23). Remember, they all (except John) had abandoned Jesus in his hour of greatest need. And Peter had denied that he even knew him. Now, locked away in a house for fear of what the Jewish authorities might do to them as his followers, they were overwhelmed with grief at the death of their lord, their master and friend, and they most likely were feeling guilty for having left him in the lurch.

Jesus came and stood among them, and said, "Peace be with you." He didn't question them. (Where were you when I needed you?) He didn't scold them for their cowardice. He didn't make them feel guilty by describing in detail all the suffering he went through without their supportive presence. He didn't question their loyalty going forward. He simply said, "Peace be with you." Conveyed in those four words was the message: All is forgiven. I love you. I need you to carry on my mission. Don't be burdened with guilt. Be at peace. In those powerful moments, the disciples experienced the meaning of reconciliation, and that is what the Sacrament of Reconciliation should be for us.

In the Sacrament of Reconciliation, as in the two Gospel incidents that I described, the focus is meant to be on Jesus and his healing, reconciling love, not on the sinner and his or her selfishness and sin. Burdened by our sin, we should sense Jesus inviting us: "Come to me, you who labor and are burdened, and I will give you rest" (Matt. 11:28). We should approach the Sacrament with eager anticipation that we will be forgiven, refreshed, and lifted up by the presence and the power of Jesus. We should come to Reconciliation with confidence that we will experience the fullness of God's love.

CHAPTER 5
So Where Is the Love?

Sadly, the focus of the Sacrament
is often on sin and the sinner
rather than on Jesus and his love and mercy.

The story is told of a priest who had just arrived at a new parish assignment. He had not even finished unpacking his bags, when he was called to lead a wake service at a local funeral home. Since he didn't know anything about the deceased, he invited those present to share: "Is there anyone here who can say something good about this man?" Silence. He went on, "Is there someone here who can say something pretty good about this man?" More silence. Again the priest asked, "Is there someone who can say anything at all that is at least somewhat positive about this man?" Finally an older gentleman stood up and said, "Well, he wasn't as bad as his brother!"

Unlike the new priest who didn't know the deceased, Jesus knows us well. He knows our goodness and our specialness. He also knows our weakness, our selfishness and sin. After all, he is always with us, in good times and in bad. Jesus knows us, and he loves us just the way we are. In the Sacrament of Reconciliation, he wants to show us how much he loves us by giving us a sign of his mercy and forgiveness, and by encouraging us to keep on going and growing in his love.

Our God longs for us to come and experience his healing love in the Sacrament. God is always waiting for us, hoping that we know how much he loves us, cares for us, and desires to shower us with love. If we Catholics only knew how much we are loved, and how much God waits to embrace us with love in the Sacrament of Reconciliation, we would flock to the Sacrament. We would be excited to come and be touched by the God of love. So why is it that so many Catholics are not drawn to the Sacrament?

Sadly, in the Sacrament of Reconciliation as we know it, the focus is more on the sinner who comes than on the God who is waiting. From the sinner's perspective, this is what the Sacrament is about:

1. I make an Examination of Conscience.
2. I confess my sins
3. I make a good Act of Contrition.
4. I accept my penance (we even speak of the Sacrament of Penance).
5. Only then do I receive absolution from the priest who ministers to me on behalf of Jesus.

It would appear that the Sacrament is basically about me and what I say and do. I go to confession. I confess in the confessional (which is now sometimes known as the Reconciliation Room). The priest confessor hears my confession. Only after all of that ritual is completed does the priest absolve me of my sins.

Some years ago, at a conference for Catholic men, I remember the master of ceremonies thanking all the priests who came to hear confessions. Wouldn't it have been inspiring and uplifting if he had thanked the priests for coming to share God's love, mercy, and forgiveness? Wouldn't it have set a wonderful tone if he had said something like this: "Jesus is here for you. Jesus loves you very much. He is anxious to forgive you and heal you through the ministry of these devoted priests. I hope you are as excited as I am to experience the presence and the power of Jesus in the Sacrament of Reconciliation."

The language and the terms that are used for the Sacrament are not particularly user-friendly:

Examination of Conscience: It sounds more clinical than pastoral. There are all sorts of lists of sins that are meant to guide our examination. In reality, we most likely already know when and how we have weakened our relationship with God and our neighbor. Using a generic Examination of Conscience can be anxiety-provoking: What does that mean? Did I do it? How many times?

Act of Contrition: Contrition is not a word we use in common conversation. "Honey, I am really contrite for yelling at you." What's wrong with calling it "a prayer of sorrow"? According to past teaching, we must be sure that we make a "good" act of contrition (as opposed to what? a bad act of contrition?). We learned about perfect contrition and imperfect contrition, and we used words like "I detest all my sins" and "I dread the loss of heaven and the pains of hell." Scary stuff! All of this is still in use for many Catholics and can be an obstacle to approaching the Sacrament.

Absolution: The priest absolves us, which, as we learned, has to do with the remission of sins. Absolution and remission are not words used in common parlance. The priest says, "Through the ministry of the Church, may God give you pardon and peace." *Pardon* is a word used commonly in the criminal justice system. What if the priest, at some point, could simply say something like this: "I forgive you of your sins, and God wants you to know that God loves you very much."

Penance: Again, it's not a word we use in common parlance. How about calling it "an act of good intention" to repair the damage done by sin, expressing a desire to do better, to make up for our selfishness, and to avoid the sin in the future?

Unfortunately, the ritual we use to celebrate the Sacrament of Reconciliation often lacks warmth and doesn't always convey clearly the love of God. It can seem very routine and generic and not be experienced as a genuine celebration of God's love. (In the parable of the prodigal son, the father called for a festive celebration for his returning son.) Even though the option should be available to sit face-to-face with the priest, many people still prefer to talk to the priest behind a screen. This method of "celebrating" can be impersonal, and the sinner does not always see the sign of forgiveness the priest offers, when he raises his hand over the sinner, indicating the coming of the Holy Spirit, and then he makes a gesture of blessing.

Today the Sacrament can still be couched in legalism. Many Catholics are reluctant to return to the Sacrament for fear of not getting it right, not remembering the right formulas or saying the right prayers. Many are afraid that they won't make "a complete confession," explaining the gravity of the sin and confessing the number of times. Judging from Jesus's relationship with sinners in the gospels, can anyone believe that Jesus would require all those details?

I can't help but think of a wonderful story, told by Father Anthony DeMello:

> "An old woman in the village was said to be receiving divine apparitions. The local priest demanded proof of their authenticity. 'When God next appears to you,' he said, 'ask Him to tell you my sins, which are known to Him alone. That should be evidence enough.'

The woman returned a month later and the priest asked if God had appeared to her again. She said He had. 'Did you put the question to Him?'

'I did.'

'And what did He say?'

He said, 'Tell the priest I have forgotten his sins.'"

(Anthony DeMello, S.J., *Taking Flight*, Doubleday, 1988)

In my judgment, God doesn't dwell on our sins. Unfortunately, the Church often tells us to dwell on our sins, to review our sins, to determine the level of seriousness of our sins, and to calculate the number of times we've committed our sins. God focuses on our basic goodness and wants to help us appreciate how good we really are at the core of our being. God wants to give us a concrete sign of his unconditional love and wants us to experience how much he delights in us. That is what the Sacrament of Reconciliation is meant to be about. That is what will bring people to the Sacrament.

CHAPTER 6
An Examination of the
Examination of Conscience

Basically, we can know what's wrong in our relationships
by listening to the voice of God within.

When it's time for you to see your primary care physician for your annual physical, you already know what issues are of concern to you: You've been having periodic stomach cramps; your right knee is hurting; you've been experiencing dizzy spells. You don't need a checklist of every possible medical condition you might have. You basically know what you need to discuss with your doctor, and you do it.

So, what is the need for an Examination of Conscience? When it's time for me to take a look at sinfulness in my life, or specifically when it is time to approach the Sacrament of Reconciliation, I should basically already know what's right and what's wrong with my relationship with God, with the people in my life, and within myself. I know what I've done that is sinful, and I know what I should be doing that I'm not doing. The "voice" of conscience speaks to me from within and helps me to understand what needs fixing in my spiritual life. On an ongoing basis, I don't need to consult a checklist of every possible sin. Such a list can be confusing and anxiety-provoking and can lead to unhealthy scrupulosity.

An examination can be helpful when a person (for example, a teenager) is learning to form a good conscience, just as training wheels can be helpful when someone is learning to ride a bike. But at some point, the training wheels will come off, and similarly, a person will learn to look at significant areas of selfishness and sin in his or her life without a checklist and will listen to the voice of conscience in the silence of the heart.

The Examination of Conscience is not specifically discussed in the Catechism of the Catholic Church, but it is mentioned in various books and pamphlets that discuss the Sacrament. I like the definition in *The Harper Collins Encyclopedia of Catholicism*, published in 1995, which refers to the Examination of Conscience as "a prayerful review of one's own life on the basis of Gospel values." A manual for instructing catechumens describes the Examination as an opportunity "to reflect on how generous our responses to God and people have been." One diocese offers "A Guide to Making a Thorough Examination of Conscience and a Good Confession." Words like *thorough* and *good* can bring on anxiety. Am I thorough, and is it good? This guide prepares you to "tell the priest the specific kind of sins you have committed and to the best of your ability how many times you have committed them since your last good confession. Avoid generalizations and inform the priest of any relevant circumstances in which your sins were committed." Most forms of the Examination that I have examined suggest that we focus on what we have done (individual sins) rather than who we have become (Have I become a generous, loving Christian or a selfish, unloving person?). I think Jesus would say, "Relax! Reflect on your life. Share what you can. Don't sweat the small stuff."

Most dioceses have a program to welcome people back to the Sacrament of Reconciliation. Some Catholics wrestle with the idea of returning to the Sacrament after many years away. They can find it a daunting task: I don't remember what to say. How can I remember all my sins after so long a time? Will the priest be understanding and compassionate with me after all that I have done wrong? The aforementioned diocesan guide uses the Ten Commandments as the basis for an Examination of Conscience. All well and good. But then there is a section entitled "Other Sins," and the first sin suggested is: "Did I intentionally refuse to mention some grave sin in my previous confessions?" I can only imagine what must go through the head of someone who sincerely wishes to return to the Lord, like the prodigal son returning home, only to be confronted with the possibility that he/she might have neglected to confess a serious sin twenty years ago. Maybe it was shame or embarrassment. Maybe it was youthful rebellion against authority. Maybe it was just the inability to see the seriousness of the situation. In any event, would Jesus expect this person to dig up something that happened so long ago? Or would Jesus simply rejoice that a lost brother or sister has come home?

Many Catholics hesitate to come back to the Sacrament, either because they don't want to dig up the past or because they are afraid that it won't be a positive experience. Will a formal Examination of Conscience point to some action or inaction that I didn't realize was a sin? Will I remember all my serious sins? Should I make a list of my sins so that I will make a "good" confession?

The story is told of a woman who suffered from scrupulosity. When she approached the Sacrament, she was always afraid that she wouldn't make a good and complete confession of her sins. Her confessor reluctantly suggested that she make a list of her sins before coming to the Sacrament. She thought that was a wonderful idea. So the next time she came to confess, she began with the traditional formula, "Bless me, father, for I have sinned. It has been three weeks since my last confession. These are my sins: a head of lettuce, a pound of thinly sliced turkey, two cans of vegetable soup ..." The priest stopped her, "Excuse me, dear lady. I think you left your sins at the supermarket."

Sadly, even today some people bring a list of their sins so they won't forget anything. Guess what: God already knows all your sins. In my judgment, God isn't interested in a complete rundown of every detail of every sin you've committed. God *is interested* in hearing you express your sorrow for sin and your desire to do better and to be closer to God. God is interested in embracing you with love and offering you forgiveness for the sins you confess and those, for whatever reason, you don't confess in detail.

Some people express the concern that they haven't really committed any sins. For example, elders will say, "What do I do at my age?" They are referring to individual sinful acts and are often talking about biggies, mortal sins, notably sexual sins. I like to say to people who question whether they sin, "Examine what's going on in your life right now, especially your attitudes. You may not have committed adultery or stolen a large amount of money or physically injured someone in a moment of rage, but are you a loving human being? Do you love others as Jesus loves you?" Little acts of unlove, impatience, or anger add up. As I like to say, "A lot of littles is a lot!" If you are a human being, you are imperfect. You can be selfish at times. If you cannot admit any selfishness, that is your sin!

As followers of Jesus, we need to understand that individual sinful acts are often not as important as ongoing sinful attitudes, attitudes like indifference or coldness of heart (As young people might say, "Whatever!" or "So what?") in the face of human need in my family, among my friends, and in the wider community. Jesus always cares for others and wants us to care as he cares!

When I am privileged to give a talk or lead a retreat or a parish renewal program, I often give participants a handout with some ideas about sinful attitudes rather than a list of individual sinful acts. (This focus can be foreign to many sincere believers.) Let me share some of these possibilities with you:

- I take God or the people in my life for granted.
- I have unreasonable expectations of people.
- I have a sense of entitlement: it's all about me—my needs and my wants.
- I don't take enough time for God, my loved ones, or myself.

- I have a closed mind about many things, including issues in the Church.
- I am materialistic. Things are a preoccupation in my life.
- I disregard many civil laws, especially behind the wheel ("Everyone does it")
- I've lost a sense of the sacred.
- I don't get angry when I should (e.g., with my children).
- I remain silent when I should speak up.
- Sports, entertainment, and social media are more important than God.
- I am indifferent to human needs among the poor, the sick, and the outcast.
- I do what "feels" right to me. I don't acknowledge objective right and wrong.
- I don't try to determine what God wants of me here and now.
- I don't believe in making real sacrifices for others who are in need.

The above list is not meant to be an Examination of Conscience but rather some ideas to stimulate our thinking about our relationship with God and with the people in our lives, ideas that will hopefully help us better understand what is our sin.

When all is said and done, the two great commandments and the one greatest commandment are basically all we need to look at in examining our conscience. Jesus said it:

> You shall love the Lord your God with all your heart, with all your soul, with all your mind, and with all your strength ... You shall love your neighbor as yourself. (Mark 12:30–31)

> Love one another as I love you. (John 15:12)

CHAPTER 7
Let Your Conscience
Be Your Guide

*Some thoughts on how I can know it is God speaking to me,
not just me speaking to myself*

In the classic film *On the Waterfront*, a dock worker, Terry Malloy, played by Marlon Brando, knows details about a murder committed by members of a corrupt longshoreman's union. Terry faces a dilemma: Does he squeal and tell authorities what he knows, thus endangering his life, or does he remain silent? He seeks advice from the local priest, played by Karl Malden. The priest says, "It's your conscience that will do the talking." Brando responds, "Conscience! That stuff will drive you nuts."

Yes, any serious effort to figure out all that conscience stuff can drive you nuts! What's right, what's wrong? What's good, what's evil? What's true, what's false? What's life-giving, what's deadly? Many a cartoon has depicted a person with an angel on one shoulder whispering into his ear, "Don't do it," and a devil on the other shoulder, whispering, "Do it."

The traditional Examination of Conscience provides us with a list of possible sins (wrongs), some of which may be relevant to our spiritual journey, while others are not. Often the traditional list will not include certain areas of selfishness (selfish attitudes more than individual sins) we need to deal with, if we are to grow in our relationship with God and with others. For example, the list may mention impatience or anger or unlove but not address the underlying problem of taking our loved ones for granted or being indifferent to their needs and concerns.

Another way for us to examine our conscience is simply to sit quietly and listen to the inner voice of God, speaking to us about God's desires for our life, directing us to live this way or that, calling us to do this or to be that. How have we responded to the Lord's call to us? How have we responded to his two great commandments: love of God and love of neighbor? How have we reached out to people in need?

Conscience is simply defined in *Webster's Collegiate Dictionary* as "an inner sense of what is right or wrong in one's conduct or motives, impelling one toward right action." Spiritually, that inner sense is the voice of God, enlightening us and directing us toward what is good and true and beautiful.

The Fathers of the Second Vatican Council, in their document on *The Church in the Modern World*, speak about conscience as that place where

> men and women discover a law which they have not laid upon themselves and which they must obey. Its voice, ever calling them to love and to do what is good and to avoid evil, tells them inwardly at the right moment: do this, shun that—Their conscience is people's most sacred core, and their sanctuary. There they are alone with God whose voice echoes in their depths. (#16)

The question is: How do I know that I am listening to the voice of God and not just listening to myself?

In his book on the formation of a Christian conscience, entitled *How Do I Know I'm Doing Right* (Pflaum Press, 1976), Father Gerard Sloyan writes,

> All of our conduct has to be held up against the measuring-stick that is Christ, not one of human law promulgated in his name. His heavenly Father and He are the ones who help us know in the Spirit what conduct is sinful. The Church tries to be helpful, not harmful, in this. Some of their sons and daughters have done harm in their attempts to help. As a whole church we must follow Christ and not them.

How do I know I'm doing right? Father Sloyan suggests some important guidelines for forming our conscience. First, we must purify ourselves of selfish inclinations—the attitude that says, "It's all about me and my wants, not about God." Fasting can be important in this regard, helping us to let go of whatever stands between us and our relationship with God—notably our selfish pursuits and pleasures (too much food, drink, texting, tweeting, shopping, accumulating, etc.). Fasting enables us to be pure of heart, opening ourselves to hear the voice of God at the core of our being.

Formation of conscience requires that we study the scriptures, especially the four gospels, where Jesus reveals to us his way, his truth, and his life. What is Jesus saying to me about this situation or that dilemma that I face? We must also consult the teachings of the Church on all levels: the teachings of the hierarchy (the magisterium) and the teachings of theologians, pastors, and faith formation programs in our parishes. We should also consult with our fellow Christians and with various people of goodwill who cross our paths. Father Richard Gula, in the *Encyclopedia of Catholicism* (Harper Collins, 1995), says, "While the judgment of conscience is always made for oneself (what I must do), it is never formed by oneself. Convictions are shaped, and obligations are learned, within the communities that influence us." For us Christians, the greatest influence is our faith community.

Formation of conscience also requires that we follow current debates on contemporary moral questions, such as war, abortion,

end-of-life issues, divorce, homosexuality, and
The bishops at the Synod on the Family in 20
in vigorous discussion on a variety of issu
consciences of the Catholic faithful. In 2016
to the bishops in his document "The Joy
attentive to all such discussion and papal teaching.

Once we have done all we can do to inform our conscience,
must ask God's forgiveness for the times when we have been self-
serving about matters of moral importance (for example, making
a decision to use artificial birth control solely because another
pregnancy would interfere with financial plans). And we must ask
for God's guidance and the wisdom of the Holy Spirit in leading us
to the truth. We must pray fervently, "Thy will be done," and then
we must sincerely seek God's will.

In St. Paul's Letter to the Romans, we read:

> I urge you, therefore, brothers (and sisters), by the
> mercies of God, to offer your bodies as a living
> sacrifice, holy and pleasing to God, your spiritual
> worship. Do not conform yourselves to this age but
> be transformed by the renewal of your mind, that
> you may discern what is the will of God, what is
> good and pleasing and perfect. (Romans 12:1–2)

For those of us who seek to do God's will in a world in which we
hear so many contrary voices, seductive voices, voices calling us to
embrace the values of materialism and consumerism, we will have to
struggle mightily to let go of our selfish desires to listen to the voice
of God. How can I resist the temptation to conform to this age that
calls us to have it all and have it now? We must open ourselves to
the presence and the power of God within us. Through the power
of God, and only through the power of God, we can be transformed
into a living witness to the way of Jesus in mind and soul and body;
we can hear his will and do his will in the conduct of our daily life.

ᴀn be overwhelming at times to deal with the conflicting ᴧnces of Church and society. What's a Christian to do? How we to hear the gentle voice of God when the voices of secularism, ᴧnd especially advertising, speak so loudly and so persuasively? Sadly, many people succumb to secular influences and don't even try to discern want God wants. I can't tell you the number of times I've heard well-intentioned people say, "I don't care what the Bible says or what the Church teaches. This is what I believe." And I answer, "If you are to consider yourself a good Catholic Christian, you must care deeply about what Jesus says and what the Church teaches as you try to form a mature conscience." In other words, we must study diligently, think deeply, and pray fervently to make right moral decisions.

The influences of society are so strong that some people cannot resist temptation, even though their conscience tells them that this or that pathway is wrong. For example, when I have counseled engaged couples who are living together before marriage, and I have tried to suggest sensitively that waiting until marriage is a better course, I not infrequently have heard the response, "Oh, I know that this living situation is not what Jesus would want, but we are good people, and God will understand." Similarly, when I have spoken out in my preaching about the gross commercialization of Christmas and have suggested that our shopping frenzy is not how Jesus would want us to celebrate his birthday, I have heard some people (especially parents) say, "Father you're absolutely right. But my family expects all the gifts and glitz, so what can I do?"

Yes, dealing with conscience can really drive a person nuts. So we must decide what is a better way of examining our conscience: Is it looking at lists of sins and trying to figure out which ones apply, or is it listening quietly to the voice of God in the sanctuary of our heart, reminding us of the basic law of love and calling us to do what is right and avoid what is wrong in the circumstances of our life?

CHAPTER 8
We All Need Encouragement

Jesus wants to encourage us to do good,
not condemn us for doing bad!

A cartoon shows two inmates discussing how they wound up in prison. One of them says, "I wrestled with my conscience—and I won."

I cannot tell you the number of times a fellow Catholic will say something like, "I wrestle with my conscience. I keep trying to do the right thing. But time and time again, I falter. I succumb to temptation. I take the selfish road. I sin. When I examine my conscience and discover the same old sinful patterns, I feel guilty. I get discouraged. I doubt the sincerity of my intentions. I question my faith in Jesus and his way. I question whether Jesus will still love me."

Some people, born of such a struggle with sin, approach the Sacrament of Reconciliation regularly, even weekly. I suspect that at least some of these people approach the Sacrament as a kind of magic potion or a spiritual shower, cleansing them of their sin, without necessarily helping them to avoid these sins in the future. Do they truly encounter a loving God in the Sacrament, or is it a God who demands endless expressions of contrition and penance?

Other people, discouraged by their recurring sinfulness, give up on the Sacrament altogether. They cannot see how the Sacrament makes any real difference in their lives. They feel like hypocrites, confessing and then committing the same sins, then returning to the Sacrament again and again. Where is our loving God making any difference in the sacramental ritual? What positive impact does God have in the life of this sinner?

Meister Eckhart, a controversial Dominican mystic and theologian in the late thirteenth and early fourteenth centuries, once made this provocative statement: "I pray to God to rid me of God." I think what he was trying to say was that if we are to grow spiritually in a healthy way, we must get rid of the unhealthy concepts and images of God that we learned in the past, some of which have crept into the Sacrament of Reconciliation.

For many people, God was the divine policeman, waiting to catch us in our sin. God was a judge, ready to condemn. God was the taskmaster, demanding a holiness we cannot achieve. God was the warden who would see to it that we were punished for our bad behavior. Those images of God were not user-friendly—a demanding God, a vengeful God, a punishing God. As a matter of fact, they were downright scary. Who would be excited to encounter such a God? The "gotcha God" was the God of our parents ("If you do that, God won't love you"), the God of some well-meaning priests and nuns, and at times, the God of our teaching Church.

I went to a Catholic high school, where I got a good education and where my vocation to the priesthood was nurtured. But I remember some frightening stories we were told about God's punishment for sin. One story, in particular, has stayed with me to this day: John and Mary were ideal Catholic teenagers. John was the president of the CYO (Catholic Youth Organization) and worked at the parish office. Mary was the vice president of the CYO and prefect of the Junior Sodality. One night, after a CYO dance, John and Mary went off together to a "lovers' lane," where they engaged in some so-called heavy petting and necking (It was adolescent passion, driven by raging hormones, but it was considered seriously sinful activity). When they got back on the highway, now burdened with their sin, their car was side-swiped by an eighteen wheeler; they were both killed instantly in the crash and were sent by God straight to hell. Ouch! I believe that many good Catholics were traumatized by such imagery and find it hard to relate to such a God.

I pray to God to rid us of that God, those harsh images of God, those frightening memories of God. As I said at the outset of these reflections, God is love, and God loves us, all of us, no matter what we have done that is contrary to God's way. God loves us as we are and not as we should be. God is with us, day in and day out; God is with us to embrace us with God's boundless love and to encourage us to be all that God knows we are trying to be. Our God is the God of encouragement, not condemnation!

Time and time again the chosen twelve apostles of Jesus struggled with their faith in this teacher, and time and time again Jesus encouraged them. The Sermon on the Mount (Matt. 5–7), a call to live a new way of life, must have left the apostles questioning whether they could embrace this radical new way. So Jesus encouraged them and reassured them by performing a series of miraculous healings in their presence. When Jesus predicted his passion and death, and then called the apostles to take up their cross and follow him (Matt. 16:21–28), they must have been anxious and totally bewildered. So, Jesus encouraged them and was transfigured before three of them, revealing himself in glory. He was in effect saying to them, "Things will turn out well. You'll see"

Jesus offered encouragement to many people in many circumstances. He cured people with serious, long-term illnesses. He raised the dead to new life. In his preaching, he encouraged countless people to have hope in his good news. Yes, our God is a God of encouragement.

In a special way, Jesus encouraged sinners. He reached out to the tax collector Zacchaeus and the woman at the well, encouraging them to turn their lives around. On the night of the resurrection, Jesus encouraged his sinful disciples who had abandoned him in his hour of need. "Peace be with you." He said it not once but twice. "Peace be with you. As I am forgiving you, now you must be my instruments of forgiveness and reconciliation for others. I need you to carry on my ministry of compassion and love. I am counting on you. You can do it. I give you my Holy Spirit to make it happen." How encouraging that must have been!

Our God is a God of encouragement. We must let go of the images of a harsh, condemning, punishing God and let God be the God who is love. We must see in Jesus the God of mercy, forgiveness, healing, and reconciliation. I think of the apostle Peter. After he had denied that he knew Jesus, not once, not twice, but three times, we can only imagine how guilty and ashamed he must have felt. Happily, after Jesus was raised from the dead, he met Peter for a one-on-one encounter at the Sea of Tiberias. Jesus didn't scold him or make him feel more guilty. Rather, Jesus encouraged Peter, inviting him to reaffirm his love for Jesus three times, and then calling him to embark on a new ministry of evangelization. "You fouled up, but that's behind us now. I need you. I trust you enough to give you some new responsibility." Words of encouragement from the God of encouragement.

And now I give you the ultimate image of the God of encouragement, presented by Jesus in the aforementioned parable of the prodigal son and his loving father. When the son returned home from his unholy adventures, his father greeted him warmly and called for a celebration. No condemnation, no insistence on an act of contrition, no talk of punishment or penance, just encouragement through a celebratory banquet. I can imagine the father talking to his wayward son later in a quiet moment, "I missed you so much. I worried about you. I prayed that you were safe. I kept wondering if there were anything I could do for you. I hoped that you would return. Now here you are. I am so happy to see you. You look a little tired and thin and bedraggled, but we will get you back to your old self. I hope you'll stay. I know we can work things out. I love you, and I'll do whatever it takes to keep you close to me. I hope you know how much I love you. I hope you know I want you to be at

home with me where you belong." Words of enco
the God of encouragement.

In the Sacrament of Reconciliation/Encourage
to share with us his love, his mercy, his healing, hi
his words of encouragement. We must let God ⸺
who is love. We must let God do his loving thing. The more we
open ourselves to the God of unconditional love, the more we will
want to be close to that loving, life-giving God. We will want to
acknowledge our sinfulness, abandon our selfishness, and embrace
God's new way of living and loving.

In the Sacrament of Reconciliation, Jesus wants to tell us three
important things:

- I love you with the fullness of my love. I love you no matter
  what. I love you in good times and in bad, when you come
  close or stay far off.
- I forgive you your sins. There is nothing you could do that
  would make me withhold forgiveness. If I could forgive
  the soldiers who killed me (and they didn't even ask for
  forgiveness), I can certainly forgive you.
- I will be with you all days as you journey through this life.
  I want to guide you, strengthen you, and encourage you
  to keep doing all the good things you do, and to avoid the
  selfish stuff.

That's what the Sacrament of Reconciliation should be all
about—an encounter with the God of encouragement.

Note: We should never take God's love for granted. God will always
love us, but God hopes and expects that we will respond to that love
by living a life of Christlike love and sacrifice and compassion.

CHAPTER 9
Bless Me, Father

Some thoughts to help the priest be
a powerful sign of God's love and forgiveness.

The story is told of a newly ordained priest who was nervous about hearing confessions, so he asked an older priest to sit with him in the confessional. When the Reconciliation time was over, the older priest offered his young colleague some suggestions.

"Look caring and concerned while the penitent confesses. Use words that suggest that you are really interested. Say things like, 'I see, yes, relax, God is with you, be at peace.' Now you try saying words like that." The young priest tried using those words and seemed pleased. Then the older priest said, "Now don't you think that's a little better than slapping your knee and saying, 'No kidding! You really did that? What happened next?'"

The role of the priest (often called the confessor) is central in the celebration of the Sacrament of Reconciliation. The priest sits in the place of Jesus. The priest is called to communicate to the penitent God's love and forgiveness, God's care and concern, by word and gesture.

The priest must approach the ministry of reconciliation as a fellow sinner. He must celebrate the Sacrament with a humble spirit, knowing that he stands on the same ground (the word *humility* comes from the Latin word for ground, which is *humus*) as the sinner who comes to receive God's mercy and forgiveness. He must acknowledge his own weakness and brokenness before God and be able to say, "I am a sinner like you." In anticipation of the 2016 Year of Mercy, Cardinal Sean O'Malley, my bishop in Boston, had this to say: "To be good confessors we (priests) must be good penitents who know that we are sinners, but that our God never tires of forgiving us and giving us another chance."

A professional social worker has told me about the background of many of the women who have abused their children. She acknowledged that, as she guided her own daughter through "the terrible twos," she realized that, given a similar upbringing as these women (often coming from dysfunctional homes, being abused themselves), she could easily have "lost it" and hurt her own daughter, just as those abusive mothers had done. That is the kind of humility the priest must have. We stand on the same ground as everyone else.

The priest must try to be a good listener. He must patiently listen as the sinner bares his or her soul, and he must try to appreciate the deeper ramification of what is being shared. (A husband might, on the surface, simply confess: "I was unkind to my wife." What he is really saying is: My wife is such a good and loving person. I know my angry words must have hurt her deeply. I am ashamed of myself for what I said to her.) We priests can be so busy and get so caught up in our many commitments that we can easily lose our focus on the penitent and be distracted by thoughts about our many other responsibilities. Focusing on the sinner and his or her individual needs requires great discipline. We must ask our loving God for the grace to be fully present to each person who comes to us.

Above all else, the priest must be present to the sinner as a lover and a reconciler, who reflects the care, the concern, and the deep compassion of our God. Pope Francis, in his Papal Bull, "The Face of Mercy," announcing 2016 as the Jubilee Year of Mercy, had this to say to priest confessors:

We priests have received the gift of the Holy Spirit for the forgiveness of sins, and we are responsible for this ... Every confessor must accept the faithful as the father in the Parable of the Prodigal Son: a father who runs out to meet his son despite the fact that he has squandered away his inheritance. Confessors are called to embrace the penitent son (or daughter) who comes back home and to express the joy of having his child back again.

It's all about God's love!

I think of Jesus at the tomb of Lazarus. The Lord was moved to tears at the death of his friend, but more importantly, I think that he wept in solidarity with Lazarus's family and friends. He felt deeply for them as they grieved the loss of their loved one. I think of Jesus weeping over the city of Jerusalem, saddened that they did not recognize God's visitation to them. Selfishly, they were blinded from seeing him as God. Unselfishly, Jesus grieved for them in their selfishness. In the same way, the priest is called to reflect the care and compassion of Jesus for all who come to the Sacrament. Penitents should take care to seek out a warm, welcoming, and Christlike priest.

I personally receive the Sacrament of Reconciliation at least three times a year, during Advent and Lent and at my annual retreat. In my experience of receiving the Sacrament, the priest/confessor has sometimes seemed uneasy meeting me face-to-face, his eyes lowered (not ever looking at me), speaking generic words of counsel, and not really making the Sacrament a personal encounter with Jesus. The priest/confessor conveys a great deal through his body language, as well as his words. He should present himself as genuinely interested and concerned to help the penitent experience the love and forgiveness of the Lord. He should even smile (really!) as he communicates with the sinner the joy of the gospel, the joy of encountering our good and merciful God.

From my own ministry of Reconciliation, I would like to share a few thoughts with my brother priests, thoughts that have guided me as I try to make the Sacrament a more meaningful experience.

When penitents first enter the Reconciliation Room, help them feel at ease. Tell them you are glad they have come and that God is especially delighted that they have approached the Sacrament. Tell them that God wants to encourage them and give them a spiritual boost. Sinners like to hear that.

Tell every penitent that our God is a loving God and has a special love for sinners. Say it very specifically: "God loves you. God loves you no matter what. There is nothing you could do that would make him love you any less." I can't count the number of times that I've told a penitent, "God loves you," and have heard them respond, "I hope so." Some people, scarred with guilt and fear from past experience, need to hear reassuring words of love again and again.

Affirm the penitents for their openness and their sincere confession of sins. Make them feel comfortable. Quoting Pope Francis, "May confessors not ask useless questions, but like the father in the parable, interrupt the speech prepared ahead of time by the prodigal son, so that confessors will learn to accept the plea for help and mercy gushing from the heart of every penitent." Tell sinners that God delights in them and embraces them with the fullness of his love, without asking them any needless or embarrassing questions.

Sometimes, when a penitent seems particularly upset by a sin and how it might affect his/her relationship with God, I will say, "Tell me something good you're doing in your life right now. God is more interested in your goodness than in your sin. God is here to encourage you to keep doing the good stuff." Such a suggestion can at first be startling to the sinner but can have a positive impact and can help people see their sinfulness in the wider perspective of their total life experience.

After the penitent confesses, offer personal words of encouragement, tailored to what the person has confessed. You might want to ask the penitent which sin is most troubling. You may then want to pause for a few seconds of silence to ask the Holy Spirit to inspire you as to what to say.

Unfortunately, many priests use certain general words of counsel, as if one size fits all. People can tell if we priests are speaking to their specific needs and concerns, rather than simply telling them to keep trying to do better, without offering any specific advice about the sin committed. For example, many men struggle with issues related to pornography on the internet. Rather than just telling them to cooperate with God's grace in a general sort of way, it might be helpful to acknowledge what a difficult situation it is, what with the ready availability of pornographic websites only a click away. Encourage them to think about ways to limit access to the corruptive websites (e.g., put the computer in an open space in the house where other family members may be present). Tell them to ask the Holy Spirit to guide them to new ways to avoid temptation. In some cases, the suggestion might be made that the penitent seek help from a therapist or by going to a meeting of Sex Addicts Anonymous. (They have a website.)

As I was preparing to write this book, I told various friends about my endeavor, and some of them gave me helpful input . One particular woman said to me, "I've been going to confession for many years, and the priest has never challenged me by asking, 'What are you going to do about it?'" The penance should be what you're going to do about it (your sin). It is important for priests to personalize the penance. The days of only "Say five Our Fathers and five Hail Marys" are hopefully gone.

The story is told about a carpenter who went to confession after he had been stealing lumber from his job site. He confessed his sins, and the priest said, "For your penance, make a novena."

The carpenter replied, "Father, I'm not quite sure what a novena is, but if you give me the blueprints, I can get the lumber."

Quite different from this humorous story, the penance should be a specific antidote to the sin committed. If a penitent confesses impatience or inappropriate anger with a family member, tell the penitent to express sorrow and to ask for forgiveness from the one who has been hurt. Tell the penitent to give the family member assurances that he/she is really trying to overcome this selfish tendency. Tell the penitent to offer a specific act of kindness for those loved ones who have been hurt.

If you feel that a prayer is the most appropriate penance, you might tell the penitent to pray for the grace to see the people he or she has sinned against as God sees them, as fundamentally good and worthy of love. Perhaps suggest that the penitent pray the Lord's Prayer just once, slowly and reflectively, pausing over specific phrases like "Give us this day our daily bread," asking for the spiritual strength to be more patient with this or that specific person. The penance should help the sinner to avoid the sin in the future.

The priest should try to be creative in giving a penance. At one Advent Reconciliation Service, I gave the penitents a sheet of paper with the following prayer and told them to focus on what they needed most from God:

Come, Lord Jesus! Bring me forgiveness.

Bring me healing.
Bring me generosity.
Bring me patience.
Bring me wisdom.

49

Bring me understanding.
Bring me honesty.
Bring me self-control.
Bring me peace.
Bring me joy.
Bring me faith.
Bring me hope.
Bring me your love.
Bring me _____ (ask for what you need).

Several penitents thanked me for the prayer and told me that they would include it as part of their regular prayer time.

The Sacrament of Reconciliation/Encouragement should be a clear sign of the presence of our loving and merciful God. The sign should be seen. In Reconciliation the sign is the priest extending his hand over the penitent, invoking the Holy Spirit, and giving the blessing of forgiveness. Unfortunately, many penitents do not clearly see the sign, since they choose to kneel behind a screen. Wherever and however possible, the priest should encourage the penitent (gently and sensitively) to receive the sacrament face-to-face, in a more personal and conversational manner, to more fully experience the power of the Sacrament. Ongoing education is needed in this regard (perhaps taking a few minutes at the end of Mass from time to time).

Sadly, since the revelation of widespread clergy sexual abuse, many priests are reluctant to get too close to the penitent to extend their hand over the penitent's head as a sign of God's healing love. Touch was an important and integral part of Jesus's ministry. He took Peter's mother-in-law by the hand. He put his finger in the deaf man's ears. He laid his hands on a crippled woman. He touched a leper. And on and on. Touch conveyed the power of the Holy Spirit, and it still does today, especially in the sacraments. We must consider ways to reach out to the penitent in a prudent way and, possibly, in a more open space. We must restore touch as an integral part of our ministry in imitation of Christ.

One final note: If the Sacrament of Reconciliation is to be a true encounter with Jesus, such an encounter will take time. If Catholics come back to the Sacrament in greater numbers, parishes must offer more opportunities for receiving the Sacrament, more than a half hour or an hour before a particular Mass on the weekend. Perhaps certain parishes could be designated as specific centers for the celebration of Reconciliation, and certain priests could be designated as special ministers of the Sacrament of Reconciliation.

> PS: If my thoughts for priest confessors make sense, you might want to share this chapter with your parish priests.

CHAPTER 10
Top Ten Reasons for Not Coming

A pastoral response to some of the major reasons
why Catholics do not approach the Sacrament

In the spirit of David Letterman's late night TV "Top Ten List,"
I offer you the top ten reasons why Catholics do not come to the
Sacrament of Reconciliation:

10. God loves me whether I go to Reconciliation or not.
9. I can tell God I am sorry by myself.
8. I don't do anything really wrong, like commit murder or
   grand theft.
7. I am not sure what is a sin anymore.
6. A priest yelled at me in the confessional many years ago,
   and I vowed I'd never go back.
5. I can't remember the formula for confession or the act of
   contrition.
4. I am afraid and embarrassed confessing to a priest.
3. My Protestant friends don't have to confess, and God
   forgives them.
2. "Love means never having to say you're sorry."
And ... the number one reason why Catholics don't come to
Reconciliation ... If I think of my sins, I feel guilty. And if I feel

guilty, I feel bad about myself. And God doesn't want me to feel bad about myself. So there!

Now let me comment on these reasons:

10. "God loves me whether I go to Reconciliation or not."

That is correct. I've said it many times in previous chapters: God loves us no matter what. God's love is unconditional. There are no ifs or buts about God's love. God would never say, "If you come to the sacraments, I will love you, but if you don't come, well that's another story." Actually God loves us so much that God wants to give us visible, concrete signs of God's love. God doesn't want us to just think about God's love, but God wants us to see and to hear and to feel the fullness of God's love and mercy in the Sacrament of Reconciliation, which is a concrete sign of healing with God and with the people in our lives.

9. "I can tell God I am sorry by myself."

Absolutely. And hopefully, as we reflect on what's gone on in our lives each day, we will want to express our sorrow to God for what was contrary to God's will for us—that is, what was sin. But the Sacrament is much more than a confession of sin. The Sacrament is fundamentally about what God wants to say to us and show us, that God loves us and forgives us and promises to be with us always, in good times and in bad. God wants to reveal God's real presence with us in the Sacrament.

8. "I don't do anything really wrong, like commit murder or grand theft."

The Church has put too much emphasis on serious individual acts, especially matters involving sexuality. Remember, a lot of littles is a lot. A regular pattern of anger or impatience or indifference, directed toward family or friends, can be as serious as one so-called mortal sin. Attitudes and patterns of sin can be as deadly as single serious acts. It is important for us to acknowledge patterns of sin as much as individual sins, to ask for God's mercy and forgiveness, and to seek God's guidance and strength to help us overcome our selfish tendencies.

7. "I am not sure what is a sin anymore."

We are living at a time of moral ambiguity. What once was clearly a sin is now not necessarily seen as a sin. For example, when I was growing up in the 1940s and '50s, the Sabbath (Sunday) was strictly observed as the Lord's Day, a day unlike the other six days of the week, a day of rest, relaxation, and spiritual renewal. We would go to Mass as a family, then come back to the house for a home-cooked family meal, then perhaps jump into the car to visit relatives or take a mystery ride to a park or the seashore. No house-cleaning or yard work or food shopping or organized youth sports. The designated day of rest was, indeed, a day of rest, unlike in recent years when Sunday has become a catch-up day, a day for accomplishing all the chores and tasks that were not done during the week. People tell me that, down deep, they know something is wrong, that they are tired and frazzled, that marriage and family life is being negatively affected. They know that Sabbath observance is one of the Ten Commandments and they are not fulfilling the command. They may not call it a sin, but they know something is wrong.

Similarly, another of the commandments prohibits killing, the taking of any human life. Yet abortion is fairly common today, for a variety of reasons. Many a woman and her partner have told me that, while they decided to have an abortion for what they considered a serious reason, they still feel they have done something wrong; they feel guilty and seek forgiveness.

Underlying the moral ambiguity that characterizes our time, people basically understand what is right and what is sin. You might want to review the chapter on conscience.

6.   "A priest yelled at me in the confessional many years ago, and I vowed I'd never go back."

Many people have told me horror stories about their experience with confession. Some people, when they were children, were truly traumatized by their moments in the dark, foreboding confessional box. I can understand why some people may find it difficult to rise above those prior experiences. If you are one of them, my suggestion to you is that you seek a kindly, sympathetic, loving priest (keep seeking until you find), and talk to him about your experience in an informal nonsacramental setting. Ask him for guidance, ask him to pray with you, and then perhaps set a time when you might celebrate the Sacrament with him. Don't let a past negative experience stop you from experiencing the love and healing of Jesus in the Sacrament here and now. Jesus greatly desires to minister to you through a loving priest. Don't reject his invitation to you because of a bad experience in the past.

5.   "I can't remember the formula for confession or the act of contrition." Formulas are not what's important. Do you think God cares if you can't remember exactly how long it's been since your last confession or you can't recall how many times you did this or that? I'm always amazed (and saddened) to hear a penitent say she was uncharitable thirty-four times. Ouch! Did she keep a tally list? There is something unhealthy about such a list. What is important is your sincere desire to experience the Lord's healing love. Let the priest know if you don't remember the formula. He will help you. Many reconciliation rooms have copies of the Rite of Reconciliation (i.e., spiritual cheat sheets). The rite includes several forms of the act of contrition, or you

can just ask God's forgiveness in your own words, for example: "Loving God, I am sorry for my sins. I will keep trying to overcome my selfishness. Please help me." Now that's easy.

4. "I am afraid and embarrassed confessing to a priest."

That is understandable. It can be embarrassing to bare your soul at Reconciliation, just as it can be embarrassing to bare your body in the doctor's office. But it is an important thing to do if you want to be spiritually or physically well. Remember: the priest is human like you. The priest is a sinner like you. He shares a common humanity with you. He is one with you, and he hopefully goes to the Sacrament like you. Just as there is a certain comfort in going to the same primary care physician for your medical needs (he or she has seen your body and knows your body), so there can also be a certain comfort and security in seeing the same priest/confessor and identifying yourself to him. He will get to know your situation and understand your struggles, and he will be able to help you grow spiritually.

3. "My Protestant friends don't have to confess, and God forgives them." There is some truth to that, but at the same time, many Protestants know that it is important to confess their sins. Some of my Protestant minister colleagues have told me that it is not uncommon for a parishioner to come to see them to talk about some sinful situation in their life and to seek forgiveness. We Catholics are blessed that we have a place where we can go at a scheduled time every week to confess our sins and experience the healing love and mercy of our God in the Sacrament. Yes, God forgives us in many ways, but the Sacrament of Reconciliation provides a special opportunity to experience God's love.

2. "Love means never having to say you're sorry." This quote, from the romantic novel *Love Story*, was used to advertise the 1970

movie version of the book. Two years later, another movie, *What's Up, Doc*, mocked that sentiment in a scene in which the Barbara Streisand character tells the Ryan O'Neal character that "Love means never having to say you're sorry," to which the O'Neal character responds, "That's the dumbest thing I ever heard." Enough said! In reality, love means wanting to say you're sorry, wanting to make up for an injury, wanting to seek healing and reconciliation. It should be that way in our relationship with a spouse or a family member or a close friend. It also should be that way in our relationship with our loving God.

1. "If I think of my sins, I feel guilty. And if I feel guilty, I feel bad about myself. And God doesn't want me to feel bad about myself. So there!"

I remember a parishioner confronting me about a challenging sermon I had given. She said, "I come to Church to feel good, and you make me feel guilty." And I responded to her, "Jesus came to us, not to make us feel good, but to help us be good." I know that many of us Catholics have been infected with "Catholic guilt," where we have been told that much of what we do is a cause for guilt. We don't want to go back to those days, but we don't want to throw out all guilt. There is such a thing as good, healthy guilt, an appreciation for what is wrong, what is truly sinful in my life. I once observed a message board in front of a Protestant church. The message read: "Guilt is a truth ache." Good guilt puts us in touch with what is true and what is false in our lives. Good guilt should make us feel good, as we confront the truth about our life and are invited to deal with that truth in a positive way.

So now that we've dealt with ten reasons why people do not approach the Sacrament, why should people come?

CHAPTER 11
So Why Come?

Four basic reasons to come to *Reconciliation*:
sacramental, scriptural, psychological, and social

Yes, there are all sorts of excuses we can use for *not* approaching the Sacrament of Reconciliation. Some Catholics will say, "I just can't see it!" Others will undoubtedly say, "I don't need it." Why, then, should we go? Let me offer four reasons for receiving the Sacrament, reasons I have often shared in my preaching and teaching.

The Sacramental Reason: Rev. Peter Gomes was a Baptist minister and chaplain at Harvard University for many years. In his book entitled *The Good Book* (Wm Morrow & Co., 1996), he affirms the value of the Catholic Sacrament of Reconciliation. He challenges us to face life squarely and admit three things: 1. Evil is real. 2. Good people are not as smart as they think they are. 3. Good people need all the help they can get to overcome evil; we cannot be good on our own. For these reasons expressed by Rev. Gomes, we need the presence and the power of Jesus in our lives as we fight the good fight in the war of the worlds, and Jesus reveals his presence in a special way in the Sacrament of Reconciliation.

I don't personally know of any Catholics who have literally heard with their own ears the voice of Jesus talking to them, forgiving them, reassuring them, encouraging them to fight the good fight against sin. A handful of holy people down through the centuries may have had such an experience, but for the rest of us, God gives us the voice of an intermediary to communicate his love and care. In the Sacrament, Jesus gives us a clear sign of his love and forgiveness, his mercy and healing, through the presence of the priest. In the Sacrament we hear the priest, and hopefully we see the priest, conveying God's presence and power, communicating God's love in a personal way. If we Catholics truly believe in the real presence of Jesus in the Sacrament of Reconciliation, we will run, not walk, to be with him and to experience his presence and the warmth of his love. As I've already suggested elsewhere, the ministry of the priest is crucial in this regard.

The Scriptural Reason: On the evening of the resurrection, Jesus came to the room where the disciples were locked away, and he stood in their midst. First, he forgave them for their cowardice and unfaithfulness, offering them the gift of peace. Then he passed the torch of forgiveness on to them, saying, "Receive the Holy Spirit. Whose sins you forgive are forgiven them, and whose sins you retain are retained" (John 20:23). He seems to be asking his followers to carry on his ministry of healing and forgiveness. It seems obvious to me that this ministry was vitally important to Jesus, given that it was the first thing on his agenda when he met his friends that Easter night. Down through the centuries, this ministry has taken on many forms, leading to the Sacrament of Reconciliation as we have it today. How blessed we are to have a place where we can come and experience the Lord's mercy, reassurance, encouragement, and guidance in a personal way through the ministry of the priest.

The Psychological Reason: As someone once said, honest confession is good for the soul. By acknowledging our human weakness, our selfishness, and our brokenness in the presence of the priest, we are saying, "I don't have it all together. I am not perfect. I have weaknesses. I am needy. I am human." Echoing the twelve steps in the AA (Alcoholics Anonymous) program, whenever I approach the Sacrament of Reconciliation, I am acknowledging that I am powerless over some aspects of my life and that I need to turn my life over to the care of a higher power, the God who can restore me to wholeness. I go to Reconciliation to admit to God, to myself, and to the priest the nature of my sinfulness. This practice is psychologically healthy and a source of healing, and it is a humbling experience.

St. Bernard, when asked to list the four cardinal virtues, answered, "Humility, humility, humility, and humility." Humility is the acknowledgment that I am on a level playing field with every other human being. At my core, I am no better or worse than anyone else. Given another set of circumstances, I could be where that person is. I think of my former archbishop, Cardinal Bernard Law, who was accused of covering up horrific cases of the sexual abuse of children by some of his priests. He was doing what most likely he believed was one of his principal duties as a bishop: to protect the pristine-pure image of the Holy Roman Catholic Church. If I had been schooled in that understanding of the bishop's role and had been put in that kind of position of authority in the Church at that time, I could possibly have done what he did. For me, that admission is humility. The Sacrament of Reconciliation affords me the opportunity to confess my common humanity, which is not perfect and can be terribly sinful. This experience is psychologically honest, humbling and healthy.

As the saying goes, the proof is in the pudding. The value of a reconciliation process is seen in the fruit that it bears. Alcoholics who embrace the twelve-step program go through a form of reconciliation:

Step 4: We made a searching and fearless moral inventory of ourselves.

Step 5: We admitted to God, to ourselves, and to another human being the exact nature of our wrongs.

Step 8: We made a list of all the persons we had harmed and became willing to make amends to them all.

Where other efforts to achieve sobriety have often failed, the twelve-step process has brought countless individuals to sobriety, wholeness, and peace. In the Sacrament of Reconciliation, our loving God wants to give us that same wholeness and a peace that the world cannot give.

The Social Reason: Every virtuous act or sinful act we perform has a social dimension. Everything we do or don't do affects not only ourselves but also our family and friends, our neighbors, and in a special way, the members of our Church. By our Baptism, we become members of the Church community, the Body of Christ. In his first letter to the Corinthians (chapter 12), St. Paul tells us: "As a body is one though it has many parts, and all the parts of the body, though many, are one body, so also Christ. For in one Spirit we were all baptized into one body … and we were all given to drink of one Spirit. If one part suffers, all the parts suffer with it; if one part is honored, all the parts share its joy."

As members of the one body of Christ, when we sin, the whole body is affected. When we succumb to selfishness, the whole body is affected. When we do something that is contrary to the way of Jesus, the whole body is affected. For example, when we are unloving or unforgiving toward a member of our family, it not only affects our immediate family, but it also weakens the faith community, the body of Christ. Therefore, it is not only important to be reconciled with that family member but also to seek reconciliation with the faith community through the ministry of the priest, who represents that community in the Sacrament of Reconciliation.

When I think of the people, and there are many, who make excuses for not doing things God's way (for example, not receiving certain sacraments), I think of Naaman, the army commander of the king of Aram, whose story is told in the second book of Kings (chapter 5). Naaman was a leper, who had suffered from the disease for some time. When he heard about the healing power of Elisha the prophet in the kingdom of Israel, he traveled to see Elisha, who, in turn, instructed Naaman to go and wash seven times in the Jordan River. Naaman resisted this instruction and went away angry, saying, "I thought that he would surely come out and stand there to invoke the Lord his God and would move his hand over the spot and thus cure the leprosy." Naaman had his own idea as to how God should operate. Happily, his servants convinced him to do as Elisha had instructed, so he washed in the Jordan and was healed.

Many Catholics have their own idea as to what God would expect of them. They will say things like, "If Jesus had come today instead of two thousand years ago, he would never tell us to love our personal enemies or to observe a day of rest in our busy world or to forgive that person who hurt us so cruelly." We can easily forget that God's ways are not our ways. We can be tempted to tell God how to be God. Like Naaman, we might be tempted to walk away.

God has his reasons for asking this or commanding that. We

must let God be God. It takes faith to let go of our way of wanting God to heal the leprosy of our sin, and to let God heal us in his wonderful ways, one of the most wonderful of which is through the Sacrament of Reconciliation. No spectacle, no drama in the Reconciliation Room. Just lots of love and a promise of peace.

CHAPTER 12
Good, Great, Awesome!

Hints for making the *Sacrament* an
awesome experience for children

Some years ago, as I was bringing God's love and forgiveness to a child in the Sacrament of Reconciliation, I said, "Jesus loves you always, when you're good and even when you do something bad. What do you think of that?"

The child answered, "That's good."

Then I said, "Jesus forgives you, no matter what sin you've committed. What do you think of that?"

The child answered, "That's great."

Then I said, "Jesus promises to be with you every day to help you be good. What do you think of that?"

And the child answered,: "That's awesome!" That child was excited and enthusiastic about encountering the love and forgiveness of Jesus in the Sacrament.

I am reminded of the incident, recorded in the gospel of Matthew (chapter 19), when children were brought to Jesus so that he might lay his hands on them and pray for them. The disciples were trying to keep them away, but Jesus said, "Let the children come to me, and do not prevent them, for the kingdom of heaven belongs to such as these." I can only imagine what a happy occasion that must have been. I picture Jesus smiling and laughing with the children, praying over them, and perhaps playing with them, showering lots of love on them. The children were undoubtedly excited and enthusiastic when they encountered the love of Jesus in their midst.

I have always been moved by Pope Francis's desire to engage personally with people in his ministry, especially when he has reached out to children. Sometimes he has stopped the Popemobile to pick up a baby, and to give a blessing and a kiss, much to the consternation of his security personnel (disciples). Sometimes he has spotted a disabled child in the crowd and has given the child a warm caress and a loving embrace. He obviously delights in the presence of children, and the children respond to him with great joy and enthusiasm. Pope Francis conveys the love, the caring, and the concern of Jesus in the way he moves among the crowds who come to see him.

When a young child comes to the Sacrament of Reconciliation, he or she should have a positive experience of a loving Jesus, like the children in the gospel story, like the children who have experienced the pope, and like the child who came to me for Reconciliation and was so enthusiastic in the presence of the Lord. Sadly, it is not always that way.

Here are a few random thoughts, gleaned from my years of pastoral ministry, about how clergy, catechists, and parents might help make the Sacrament of Reconciliation a more inviting and more relevant experience for our children:

The Words We Use: Reconciliation, examination of conscience, act of contrition, absolution, penance—these do not speak to school-age children. We must explore the use of new words that speak to our young people:

"Making peace with those we've hurt," instead of reconciliation.

"Thinking about our sins," instead of an examination of conscience.

"Telling God we are sorry," instead of an act of contrition.

"Forgiving the sin," instead of absolution.

"Doing something good to make up for the bad things we've done," instead of a penance.

The Formula for Receiving the Sacrament: Children may not easily remember the words to say and when to say them. I don't think that it is critical for a child to say how long it's been since the last confession, yet that is part of the formula they learn.

I remember one child, at his *first* Reconciliation, saying, "Bless me, Father, for I have sinned. It has been two weeks since my last confession." That was the formula he had learned, so he said it. Very often, a child will forget the formal Act of Contrition. I believe that it is sufficient for a child to say, "Jesus, I'm sorry for my sins. I'll try to do better."

Teach Children What Is a Sin in Their World: We must keep it simple, helping them to understand the sinfulness of things they can relate to, like disobeying, fighting, hurting feelings, lying, stealing, cheating, refusing to share or to help. In my judgment, it makes no sense to teach grammar school children the Ten Commandments, when they cannot relate to sins like adultery, bearing false witness, and coveting.

Many years ago there was a fourth-grade child who had just been taught the Ten Commandments. He figured that, since they were the ten biggies, he must have sinned against them. So he began his confession of sins by saying, "Bless me, Father, for I have sinned. I covered my neighbor's wife four times ..." Ouch! It makes no sense to teach children ideas and moral norms that they cannot possibly comprehend.

Keep the Celebration of the Sacrament Just That—a Celebration: I can't tell you how many times I've participated in a first Reconciliation service, where I've heard the pastor tell the children, "There's nothing to be afraid of." You only tell someone that there's nothing to be afraid of when there is potentially something to be afraid of.

At other times, I've heard the pastor say, "There's nothing to worry about. No one's going to yell at you." When a parent brings a child to a classmate's birthday party, the parent most likely doesn't say, "There's nothing to worry about." You only tell a child, "No one's going to yell at you," when there is the concern that someone is going to yell at you. Clergy, catechists, parents: keep it positive! Tell the children in your charge that the Sacrament is a beautiful, wonderful, joyful meeting with Jesus through the help of his friend, the priest. We must not scar our children with *our* fears, *our* worries, *our* bad experiences.

Also, tell the children, "It's okay if you forget exactly what to say." The formal words aren't all that important. What is important is that the children simply tell Jesus that they are sorry for the sins they mention. Too much time is spent in drilling the children in the formulas for Reconciliation. Don't overemphasize the formalities with the children. Keep it simple. Keep it upbeat. Keep it special.

Once, when I noticed that a child was particularly nervous sitting with me for first Reconciliation, I asked, "Are you nervous?"

The child responded, "Yes, I've been up all night thinking about this."

It shouldn't be that way. I hope and pray that, in the future, if we ask our children how they feel about coming to the Sacrament, they will say, "I'm excited. I'm happy. It's awesome."

Have a Practice Session for Face-to-Face Reconciliation: In my effort to take away the fear factor from the children as I prepared them for Reconciliation, I would have a "practice session" in a large assembly, for all the children and their parents. The session would be a happy, joyous time, containing the following elements:

1. I would talk informally about the Sacrament, emphasizing that it is a celebration. I would try to say things to make the children smile and laugh and feel at home.
2. I (or a cantor) would lead them in some singing. I would get them going, clapping and swaying, with a song like, "If you're happy and you know it, clap your hands ..." We would also rehearse the *simple* hymns to be used at the celebration of the Sacrament. I emphasize the word *simple* since I've often participated at first Reconciliation services where the words and the melody were not specifically suited to children. There are many good children's hymns available.
3. Then I would ask for volunteers to come up front and sit face-to-face with me, and we would go through a practice version of the Sacrament. I would tell them, "Just make up some sins, like disobeying, or fighting with your brothers and sisters, or telling lies." Of course, these were the very kind of sins they would confess for real. Then I would talk to them, just as I would do in the Sacrament, and tell them how much God loves them. The kids really seemed to enjoy it. So many of them volunteered to come up that I couldn't

accommodate them all. No fear, no self-consciousness—just a happy time together with me and Jesus. May it ever be so!

Celebrate First Reconciliation in a Family Setting

– Make it a real celebration, like the celebration ordered by the father to celebrate the return of his prodigal son.
– Decorate the front of the church with colorful posters (made by the children) and perhaps some helium-filled balloons.
– Keep the celebration upbeat, with lively hymns that everyone knows. Emphasize how exciting it is to be with Jesus, who loves us and forgives us.
– Perhaps involve the children in a dialogue homily, *or* have an impromptu dramatization of the return of the lost sheep. I have often done something like this:

> Ask for a child to volunteer to be the lost sheep, named Wooly, who wanders to the back of the church.

> Ask for another child to be Shep, the Ship-Shape Shepherd, who searches for Wooly.

> Invite a number of children to be the ninety-nine sheep, who will welcome Wooly home with sanctuary bells and noise makers and streamers and cheers and a song (to the tune of "Happy Birthday"): "Welcome home, we love you. Welcome home, we love you! Welcome home, our dear Wooly. Welcome home, we love you!"

The children can really get into the welcoming, and it can create a lot of genuine enthusiasm.

When it is time for individual Reconciliation, the parent(s) might be invited to present the child to the priest. The parent(s) might also be invited to receive the Sacrament before or after the child as a sign that the Sacrament is not just a discipline for children. We all need a sign of God's forgiveness and love.

When the celebration of Reconciliation has ended, children and parents might be invited to the parish hall for a mini party. In recent years I have been pleasantly surprised at the number of families that took pictures of the priest and the child at the party—a permanent memory of a genuine celebration.

CHAPTER 13
The Unconfessed Sins

Apathy and indifference in the face of human need
and suffering are rarely confessed as sins, but they are.

"Bless me, Father, for I have sinned. I saw news reports of refugees
fleeing from bloody conflict. I saw them walking for miles and
miles along dirt roads with nothing but the clothes on their backs.
I saw them carrying tiny infants in their arms or fragile elders on
their backs. I saw the deplorable conditions in the refugee camps.
I saw many refugees fleeing in overcrowded boats, and I learned
that some of the boats had capsized. I saw the image of a little boy
who drowned and was washed up onto a beach. I saw, I heard, and
I did nothing! And I never even tried to find out whether there was
something I could do." Such indifference is a sin, what we call social
sin—that is, apathy and inaction in the face of societal injustice.

In my fifty-plus years as a Roman Catholic priest, I have seldom,
if ever, heard anyone confess that they were indifferent in the face
of human tragedy. I cannot remember anyone admitting that they
turned a blind eye to the needs of the poor, the homeless, the weak,
the outcasts, or the victims of war, human trafficking, the drug
trade, and various natural disasters. At the same time, I rarely see
social sin mentioned in the traditional list of sins published in various
forms of the examination of conscience.

We are a human family. We call God Father (some people call

God Mother). "God created man (and woman) in his image; in the divine image he created him; male and female he created them ... God looked at everything he had made, and he found it very good" (Genesis 1). Every human being on planet earth is a member of the human family and is, at the core, very good. Every member is precious in God's sight. We are all related to one another as brothers and sisters. We are responsible for one another. We are our brothers' and sisters' keeper. We are called to promote the dignity of all and justice for all.

"Bless me, Father, for I have sinned. I have read reports about the problems in our inner cities. I have watched the news on TV, and I have seen the aftermath of poverty, violence, and racism. I have seen the homeless huddled together on the city streets in the midst of freezing cold winter weather. I have read the reports and seen the pictures, and I have basically said, 'That's not my concern, not my problem.' Sometimes I have even harbored prejudice or discrimination toward these needy people and toward many people who are different from me."

Jesus tells us that the needs of our brothers and sisters must be our concern. He said, "Love one another as I have loved you." Jesus loved everyone, especially those in need, with the fullness of love. He also said, "Love your neighbor as yourself." So who is our neighbor? Jesus gave us the answer by telling us the parable of the Good Samaritan, the story of a man who risked his life and shared his wealth to care for a complete stranger who had been attacked and left for dead. Jesus ended the story by saying, "Go and do the same" (Luke 10:30–37). If we don't do the same, that is our sin.

Pope Francis, in his 2015 document entitled "The Face of Mercy," in which he announced an Extraordinary Jubilee (Year) of Mercy, had this to say:

> It is my burning desire that, during this Jubilee,
> the Christian people may reflect on the corporal
> and spiritual works of mercy. It will be a way to

reawaken our conscience, too often grown dull in
the face of poverty. And let us enter more deeply
into the heart of the gospel where the poor have a
special experience of God's mercy. Jesus introduces
us to these works of mercy in his preaching so that
we can know whether or not we are living as his
disciples.

In a special way, the Holy Father has called us to rediscover
the corporal works of mercy: to feed the hungry, give drink to the
thirsty, clothe the naked, welcome the stranger, heal the sick, visit
the imprisoned, and bury the dead. There are people with various
kinds of poverty, scarcity, and want, who need our help.

You might be tempted to say to yourself: "What can I do to
help these people? I don't personally know anyone who goes without
basic human needs." And I say to you: Couldn't you at least take
time to learn about global and local social issues? Couldn't you
actively support individuals and organizations that are working to
alleviate human suffering and injustice? Couldn't you investigate
whether there is a need for volunteers at your local food pantry or
homeless shelter or Meals on Wheels program? Couldn't you host
a foreign exchange student or a family that was left homeless after
a natural disaster? Couldn't you find out what are the pressing
concerns at Catholic Charities or Catholic Relief Services or one of
many other aid organizations? Couldn't you contact the chaplain
at a local prison and find out if there is an inmate who never has a
visitor? Couldn't you ask at your local parish if there is a shut-in who
might appreciate the help of a fellow parishioner who could do some
shopping or provide a ride to a doctor's visit? If you won't consider
any of these possibilities, even though you have the time and energy
to do something, then maybe that is your sin. Apathy in the face of
human need is a sin.

Many years ago I heard a song entitled "The Shortest Story,"
written by Harry Chapin. It is about the life of a baby born in a

country ravaged by famine. In the first verse, the baby is born, draws its first breath, and seems glad to be alive. In the second verse, on its seventh day of life, the baby experiences extreme hunger, as its mother's breast provides no milk. And then comes the tragic third verse:

> It is twenty days today, Mama does not hold me anymore.
> I open my mouth, but I am too weak to cry.
> Above me a bird slowly crawls across the sky.
> Why is there nothing now to do but die?

We've all seen pictures of starving children, their ribs almost bursting forth from their chests. We've seen the pictures of their parents—helpless, desperate, grieving, as they watch their children slowly die. We've seen, but what do we do? Many of us will contribute a few dollars in a special collection at church, but soon we forget the images and move on with our comfortable lives. We even forget to pray regularly for our needy brothers and sisters beyond the occasional petition in the Prayer of the Faithful at Mass. Perhaps that forgetfulness is our sin. For me, that song, "The Shortest Story," has challenged me never to forget.

Pope Francis also called us to remember the spiritual works of mercy: to counsel the doubtful, instruct the ignorant, admonish sinners, comfort the afflicted, forgive offenses, bear patiently with those who do us ill, and pray for the living and the dead. Let's be honest: we all know someone who needs one or more of these spiritual works. To neglect them in their spiritual need may be our sin.

As Christians and as members of the human family, we must reflect carefully and prayerfully about the works of mercy, especially about our relationship to the hungry and the homeless, refugees and strangers, the weak and the suffering, the victims of war and civil unrest. In Matthew 25, Jesus tells us that, at the end of this life, we will be judged on how we respond or don't respond to those in need. He speaks in a parable about sheep and goats: The sheep (the followers of Jesus' way) have reached out to the hungry, the thirsty, the stranger, the naked, the ill, the prisoner, and our brothers and sisters in whatever need. Jesus congratulates them, tells them that their active love of the needy is, in effect, love of Jesus himself, and he gives them an eternal reward. The goats, on the other hand (those who did not follow Jesus's way), will be punished. This parable is a stark reminder that active, selfless, all-embracing love of our brothers and sisters in need is basically what authentic Christian life must be about.

In his announcement of the jubilee of mercy, Pope Francis expressed the hope that we Christians will think about the works of mercy, reawaken our conscience to the plight of the needy, and then determine whether we are truly living as disciples of the Lord. The Sacrament of Reconciliation can provide us with a wonderful opportunity to do just that, and to seek God's forgiveness for those times when we have failed.

CHAPTER 14
We're All in This Together

A consideration of the value of a Communal *Reconciliation* Service

Some years ago, I was given the opportunity to take a break from my parish ministry to participate in a sabbatical program for priests. The three-month program included daily classes on various theological and pastoral topics. We also had the opportunity to receive spiritual direction, to go on a directed retreat, and to join a weekly support group, facilitated by a psychologist, where each of us could share our personal experience of priesthood and discuss various psychological issues facing us as flesh-and-blood human beings.

That support group was a powerful experience. Most participants were open and transparent in sharing their stories. We shared our joyful experiences in bringing the good news of Jesus to countless people in our care, and we shared our struggles with issues such as celibacy, Church authority, and rectory living. The sharing was almost like an open confession, as we admitted that, at times, we had failed to live up to our priestly calling. For me personally, the sharing was especially uplifting as I recognized that we priests are all in the same boat, dealing with similar struggles, and needing mutual encouragement and support. I was relieved to find out that I am a sinner among fellow sinners in the ministerial priesthood.

My experience on sabbatical reminds me that all of us baptized Christians are sinners, in need of the mercy and forgiveness of Jesus, and also in need of the support and encouragement of our fellow members in the Body of Christ, the Church. We are all on this journey of faith together. We all struggle to follow the way of Jesus. Sometimes we succeed; sometimes we do not. At times we can be self-centered and self-serving. We can wander off to do our own thing. We need the love of Jesus and the support of our brothers and sisters to help us get back on track.

I am reminded of a story by Martin Bell in his book entitled *The Way of the Wolf,* Seabury Press, 1968. The story is called "The Ragtag Army," and it begins like this:

> "I think that God must be very old and very tired. Maybe he used to look splendid and fine in his general's uniform, but no more. He's been on the march a long time, you know. And look at his ragtag little army! All he has for soldiers are you and me. Dumb little army. Listen! The drum beat isn't even regular. Everyone is out of step. And there! You see? God keeps stopping along the way to pick up one of his tinier soldiers who decided to wander off and play with a frog, or run in a field, or whose foot got tangled in the underbrush. He'll never get anywhere that way. And yet the march goes on.

We Christians are God's ragtag army. We are fighting the spiritual warfare raging in our world today. We are clothed in the armor of God (God's grace). We "take the helmet of salvation and the sword of the spirit, the word of God" (Galatians 6). And we are fortified with the only weapon that can finally win the battle, God's unconditional, all-embracing love. We are marching together with our brothers and sisters in Christ, but sadly, at times one or another of us can wander off from the group, get tangled in the underbrush of our society, and succumb to the powers of this world. Just as my priest support group in California offered guidance and encouragement to each member of the group, so our parish community is called, in the spirit of Jesus, to help renew and revitalize its members when they go astray, lose their way, or feel they don't belong.

In the years since the Second Vatican Council, the Catholic Church has offered a new way to celebrate the Sacrament of Reconciliation within the context of a communal prayer service. We might look at it as a support group for sinners, or we could describe it as a meeting of SA (Sinners Anonymous). Many parishes offer such a communal celebration during Advent and Lent. It is a wonderful way for us to recognize that we are all on this spiritual journey together, that we all falter or fail from time to time, and that we all can be a source of strength and encouragement for one another.

At a communal celebration, we pray together and we sing together. There are some wonderful hymns in which we celebrate the presence of our loving and forgiving God and we address our need for God's saving love. Here are a couple of my favorites:

> *Save us, O Lord*; carry us back. Rouse your power
> and come. Rescue your people; show us your face.
> Bring us back.
> —Bob Dufford, S.J., 1981

> *Loving and forgiving* are you, O Lord; slow to anger,
> rich in kindness, loving and forgiving are you.
> —Scott Soper, 1992

How powerful it is when we express together our faith in our loving God and our need for God's forgiveness in our lives. We're all in this together!

At a communal service, we listen together to a proclamation of God's word and we reflect on that word, knowing that we are all like the lost sheep or the prodigal son in one way or another. After a few moments of quiet reflection, a minister of the service will lead the assembled sinners to a consideration of our sin, not an exhaustive list of sins, but a few possible areas of sinfulness to jump-start everyone's thinking about their sin. How encouraging it is to realize that we all have been guilty of one or more of the sins mentioned. Then, together we pray an act of sorrow. This can be one of the most powerful moments in the service, as we acknowledge together our sinfulness, our sorrow, and our desire to be better. Yes, we're all in this together.

At this point in the service, the assembled sinners are invited to approach one of the priests who are present for an individual celebration of Reconciliation. The community should be told that, since this is a communal service, each penitent should make a simple confession of sin (no unnecessary details, not a time to seek counseling), and the priest will then offer the simple prayer of forgiveness. While these individual celebrations of Reconciliation are happening, the entire congregation should be encouraged to pray for one another as a sign of support and spiritual friendship.

As for the penance at a communal service, it can be powerful to do a communal penance. For example, when individuals complete their celebration of Reconciliation, they might be directed to sit in a designated area. When eight or ten people are seated there, a minister (deacon, pastoral associate, etc.) will invite them to come around the altar to pray together a psalm of praise and thanksgiving or some other suitable prayer. Then they might be invited to share a sign of peace and encouragement. This can be a meaningful way to end the service, although people might be encouraged to stay for a final prayer and hymn after all celebrations of individual Reconciliation have ended.

Some Catholics cannot bring themselves to receive individual Reconciliation. There are many reasons for this: shame, embarrassment, guilt, feelings of unworthiness, a prior traumatic experience in confession, or a lingering doubt about the value of the Sacrament. For these Catholics, the communal service can be a wonderful opportunity to reflect on their sinfulness, to express their need for God's forgiveness and grace, and to make an act of sorrow in community with their brothers and sisters. It can also be a relief for each of the assembled sinners to recognize that he or she is a sinner among fellow sinners in the Body of Christ. As those who are reluctant to confess sit quietly and observe their brothers and sisters approach one of the priests, it might inspire them to go to Reconciliation themselves. Some individuals have told me that this is what happened to them. The communal service can truly be a grace-filled experience.

Every once in a while, I'll be at a gathering of friends or fellow Catholics, where the subject of Reconciliation will come up, and some lively conversation will ensue. Many people have questions, concerns, and objections related to the Sacrament. Providing them with a time and place to speak frankly about their issues and listen to others can help them to see the Sacrament in a new perspective. We're all in this together, so we need the support of one another to help us appreciate the value of Reconciliation as a wonderful encounter with our loving and forgiving God.

CHAPTER 15
Make Me an Instrument of Your Peace

We are all called to bring God's healing and forgiveness to those who need it

"I bet you don't know the Lord's Prayer," a young boy challenged his friend.

"I bet I do," the friend replied.

"I'll bet you a dollar you don't."

"I'll bet you five dollars I do."

"Okay, let's hear it."

"Now I lay me down to sleep. I pray the Lord my soul to keep. If I should die before I wake, I pray the Lord my soul to take."

"All right, here's your five dollars. I didn't realize you knew it."

We Christians know the Lord's Prayer and have prayed it countless times. We have prayed the prayer, but have we truly embraced the meaning of the prayer? For example, we pray, "Forgive us our trespasses as we forgive those who trespass against us." But have we truly embraced a spirit of forgiveness toward those who have hurt us?

My reflections in this book have focused on God's mercy and forgiveness toward us. I have also looked at the role of the priest as the instrument of God's forgiveness in the Sacrament of Reconciliation.

In this chapter I want to focus on the ministry of all Christians as instruments of mercy and reconciliation. When Jesus said, "Love one another as I have loved you," he was speaking to all those who would follow him. He was also telling us, by implication, that we should forgive one another as he forgives us.

Yes, the ministry of reconciliation is for all Christians and not just for priests. *The United States Catholic Catechism for Adults* (USCCB, 2006) tells us:

> By Baptism every member of the Church participates in Christ's role as priest, prophet, and king ... The laity do this in the context of their lives within families, parish communities, civic communities, and the workplace. The everyday gift of themselves in love and care for others, often done at great personal cost, is a priestly offering that is joined to the sacrifice of Christ in the Eucharist ... The laity are in the unique position of being able directly to infuse culture and society with the Gospel. (page 134)

The Catechism is telling us that all Roman Catholics, clergy and lay, are called to share in the ministry of Jesus, which includes the ministry of forgiveness and reconciliation.

The ministry of forgiveness can be tough stuff when we come face-to-face with people who have maligned us, shunned us, or hurt us as individuals or as a community. Some people would say that, in certain circumstances, it is impossible to forgive. I think of the response of the angel to the virgin Mary when Mary questioned the possibility that she could become pregnant: "Nothing will be impossible for God" (Luke 1:37). And I remember the old saying, "To err is human; to forgive is divine." We Christians have within us the divine power of God through our Baptism. With that power, forgiveness is always possible.

Some years ago, I started a scrapbook of stories and news clippings about men and women who offered extraordinary forgiveness. I titled my scrapbook: *It Can Be Done!* Here are some entries:

> Mary McDougald said she prayed that the slaying of her son does not lead to more bloodshed. Mary said that she wanted to send a message to the people who killed her youngest son: choose God and life instead of guns, drugs, and death. "If I saw them, I would have to tell them that I love them and that God loves them more."

> Terry Anderson was held hostage in Lebanon from 1985 to 1991. Asked for comment about his captors, Terry said, "I am free. I do not hate them. I am certainly not grateful to them for anything. I believe they are very wrong. They did great harm to me and to my family … I am a Christian and a Catholic. It is required of me that I forgive no matter how hard that may be. I am determined to do that."

> In *Dead Man Walking* by Sister Helen Prejean C.S.J. (Vintage Books, 1993), she tells a story about Lloyd LeBlanc, whose son was murdered by Patrick Sonnier: "He says that when he arrived with sheriff's deputies there in the cane field to identify his son, he had knelt by his boy—'laying down there with his two little eyes sticking out like bullets'—and prayed the Our Father. And when he came to the words: 'Forgive us our trespasses as we forgive those who trespass against us,' he had not halted or equivocated, and he said, 'Whoever did this, I forgive them.'"

Jesus told us that we must love our enemies and pray for those who persecute us. We must love global evildoers, terrorists, and all who would do us harm. We must love our personal "enemies": the fellow employee who used devious means to get the promotion I had hoped for, the neighbor who plays loud music day and night and refuses to turn down the volume, the sibling who manipulated Mom or Dad to get the largest share of the inheritance, the parishioner who spread a nasty rumor about my personal life.

During the days when a Boston jury was deliberating about the sentence for the marathon bomber, I heard a number of people, including Catholics, say that they hoped he would not get the death penalty, but would rather "rot in jail for the rest of his life." In the face of such hateful talk, we Christians have an opportunity to proclaim the love of God for all people. When we are chatting during a coffee break or at a social gathering and the conversation turns to controversial issues, like water-boarding of prisoners or the exclusion of refugees from our country or the stereotyping of Muslims in our society, we Christians are called to respond as Jesus would respond, witnessing to his all-embracing, unconditional love. We are called to remind our brothers and sisters that Jesus reached out to enemies and foreigners and people of various religious traditions and wants us to do the same.

On the night of the resurrection, when Jesus met with his disciples, he not only forgave them for abandoning him, but he also commissioned them to be stand-ins for him in carrying on his ministry of forgiveness and reconciliation (John 20:19–23). He said to them, "Receive the Holy Spirit. Whose sins you forgive are forgiven them ..." Every time we listen to that gospel passage, since it is the living word of God, God is speaking to all of us, not just to priests. God is forgiving us, empowering us with his Spirit, and calling us to carry on his ministry of mercy and forgiveness. God is calling us to practice the spiritual works of mercy: admonishing the sinner, forgiving offenses, and bearing patiently with those who would do us ill. To everyone we meet, we must say with Jesus, "Peace be with you."

As followers of Jesus, we Christians are called to embrace the Prayer of St. Francis as the blueprint for forgiveness and peace. In a world in which there is so much hatred, injury, doubt, despair, darkness, and sadness, we might pray this adaptation:

Lord, make us instruments of your peace.

Help us sow seeds of your boundless *love* in the hearts of all who are hateful.

Help us give the gift of *pardon* and forgiveness to all who have caused harm.

Help us share our *faith* in a loving God with all who question God's love and forgiveness.

Help us bring new *hope* to all who see their life situation as hopeless.

Help us shine the *light* of new possibilities on all who are couched in darkness.

Help us radiate the *joy* of the gospel in our world that is filled with so much gloom and doom.

Lord, fill us with your Spirit, that we may be instruments of your peace.

Amen.

While we as Christians are called to love and forgive and pray for those who have caused grave harm, we must also acknowledge that they should receive some kind of punishment for their sins, but in a life-giving and redemptive way.

CHAPTER 16
Some Final Tidbits

The following story comes from the book *A World of Stories*, by Father William A. Bausch (Twenty-Third Publications, 1998). A husband told Father Bausch this story about his wife:

> I remember a time when I was sitting on the antique window seat that Helen had treasured through the years. Because the original fabric had worn through, Helen had recently re-covered it in a handsome corduroy. A heavy storm was in progress, and I sat staring at the rain pelting down on dead autumn leaves. The gloomy look of the garden seemed to match the mood of hopelessness that had come over me. Problems at work had made me fearful of the future. Basic questions that surface with the coming of middle-age had made me fearful of life itself.
>
> I started to light my pipe and accidentally spilled some hot ash which burnt a hole right in the center of the window seat cover. Seeing what had happened, Helen calmly threaded a needle and stitched a beautiful flower over the charred spot. When I looked at the finished work, I realized that it was a striking symbol of our long life together, and

my spirits began to soar. I had married a repairer of broken spirits, a healer of wounds, a woman whose very presence was an antidote to fear. Moreover, I understood, perhaps for the first time, that it was Helen's deep and abiding trust in God's goodness that made it possible for her to be a source of light and a harbinger of hope in times of darkness and despair.

The husband's description of his wife reminds me of Jesus, who came to live with us two thousand years ago and who is with us today—a repairer of broken spirits, a healer of wounds, an antidote to fear, a source of light, and a harbinger of hope in times of darkness and despair. Jesus stitches the flower of his boundless love over the burnt hole of our selfishness and sin, a love that brings forgiveness and healing, bringing it in a special way in the Sacrament of Reconciliation, making of us something beautiful. That unconditional love of Jesus enables us to be, like Helen, an instrument of Christ's healing and mercy and peace for others.

God is love. These are the words from St. John's first letter with which I introduced the theme of this slender volume. God's love is everlasting ... really! There is nothing any of us could do that could cause God to love us any less. In this regard I want to share with you some powerful words from Soren Kierkegaard, the Danish philosopher and theologian:

> This is all I have known for certain, that God is love.

> Even if I have been mistaken about this or that point, God is nevertheless love.

> If I have made a mistake, it will be plain enough; so I repent—and God is love.

He is love—not He was love, nor He will be love, oh no, even that future is too slow for me – He is love.

Oh, how wonderful! Sometimes, perhaps, my repentance does not come at once, and so there is a future.

But God keeps no person waiting, for He is love.

Like spring water which keeps the same temperature summer and winter—so God is love. His love is a spring that never runs dry.

In Summary

Throughout this book, I have stressed the presence of a God who loves us as we are and not necessarily as we should be, a God who is always waiting for us to come home, with our sins and our burdens, with our goodness, our hopes, and our dreams. Our God is waiting to shower us with the fullness of love; God wants to embrace us with mercy and forgiveness and peace.

I am reminded of the words of a beautiful song by Paul Garr, an Australian composer:

> Come as you are, that's how I want you;
> Come as you are, feel quite at home,
> Close to my heart, loved and forgiven.
> Come as you are; why stand alone.
>
> No need to fear, love sets no limits;
> No need to fear, love never ends.
> Don't run away, shamed and disheartened.
> Rest in my love; trust me again.

There you have it. God is love. He is our repairer of broken spirits, our healer of wounds, our source of light, and our harbinger of hope. God is always waiting for us to come home to him. God wants to enfold us with his love and mercy, and God wants to reveal this love in a special way in the Sacrament of Reconciliation.

So come on home and experience the God who is love!